COVENTRY CITY

A CLUB
WITHOUT A
HOME

THE FIGHT BEHIND THE SKY BLUES'
RETURN FROM EXILE

COVENTRY CITY

A CLUB WITHOUT A HOME

THE FIGHT BEHIND THE SKY BLUES' RETURN FROM EXILE

SIMON GILBERT

First published by Pitch Publishing, 2016

Pitch Publishing'
A2 Yeoman Gate
Yeoman Way
Worthing
Sussex
BN13 3QZ
www.pitchpublishing.co.uk
info@pitchpublishing.co.uk

A CIP catalogue record is available for this book
from the British Library.

ISBN 978-1-78531-210-6

Typesetting and origination by Pitch Publishing
Printed by Bell & Bain, Glasgow, Scotland

Contents

Acknowledgements

THIS book would not have been possible without the support and encouragement of my beautiful pregnant wife, Carly. Her patience was stretched to the limit as I spent countless days and nights hunched over a laptop rather than giving her the attention she deserves.

I would also like to thank my soon-to-be-born son for inspiring me to produce something I hope he will be proud of when he's old enough to understand.

Thanks to my parents, family and friends for offering words of motivation when there seemed to be no end in sight.

Some gratitude also goes to my loyal canine companion, Tippy, who was always there with a smile on her face and a wag in her tail whenever my spirits waned.

There is special appreciation for the efforts of Robert Seeley and Daniel Gill, who tore through the first draft in record time.

Thank you to those interviewed for the book: Alan Payne, Bob Ainsworth, Bryan Richardson, Carl Baker, David Conn, Gary Hoffman, Geoffrey Robinson, James Whiting, Joe Elliott, John McGuigan, Jan Mokrzycki, Jordan Clarke, Paul Fletcher, Peter Knatchbull-Hugessen, Steve Brown and Steven Pressley.

Thanks also to Mark Labovitch and Tim Fisher for providing some excellent narration over the years.

I would also express my eternal gratitude to former Coventry Telegraph editor Alun Thorne who hired me and provided the backing needed to report a challenging and complicated subject – often in hostile conditions.

That support has continued under the editorship of Keith Perry, who has enabled me to take undisputed ownership of this subject.

Thank you to many of my current and former colleagues at the *Coventry Telegraph,* who have been forced to pick up the slack when my energies were focused on CCFC – or sub-edit the thousands of words of copy filed on this subject.

Appreciation also goes to Trinity Mirror for allowing me to use the archived news coverage in the *Coventry Telegraph.*

Further thanks to Steve Phelps, who has helped steer me in the right direction as I took my first steps into the world of becoming an author.

Thanks also to Duncan Olner for the cover design as well as Paul and Jane Camillin and the entire Pitch Publishing team for putting their faith in me to deliver this title.

But, most of all, thanks to the Sky Blue Army. I'm your biggest fan.

Chapter One

Goodbye Highfield Road

HOW did we get here? A question all too familiar to Coventry City FC supporters who find their team languishing in the third tier of English football and with no ground to call their own.

This once-proud club, with over 130 years of history and 34 consecutive years in the English top flight, has ultimately ended up homeless. At one point, the club even left Coventry for over a season but, thanks in no small part to the passion of its fans, the club has at least returned to its home city.

But where did it all go wrong?

In order to provide the answers, we have to go back almost 20 years to the very beginning of the club's modern-day problems.

In 1997, Coventry City FC chairman Bryan Richardson unveiled his vision for the future of the Sky Blues.

His idea was undoubtedly ground-breaking, ambitious and exciting. But it also carried huge risks – risks Sky Blues fans are still paying the price for today.

At the time, few spoke out against the plans for a flashy new stadium complete with sliding roof and retractable pitch. As supporters, we were dazzled by the prospect of what could be and promises that Coventry City FC would be self-sustainable, with the income needed to build a world-class team and compete with Europe's elite.

But, with the benefit of hindsight, it's a different story today.

It's easy to see why so many of us were taken in. This was a period when the club was spending money like never before. A board led by Richardson, supported by Mike McGinnity and Derek Higgs and bankrolled by Geoffrey Robinson, had put their money where their mouths were in a bid to take Coventry City into Europe.

Footballers recognised across the globe donned the sky blue of Coventry City. It was a period when the team was graced by glittering international stars such as Robbie Keane, Gary McAllister and Mustapha Hadji.

Life as a Coventry City fan was good back then – and Richardson had promised things were about to get a whole lot better.

Highfield Road was a much-loved ground, but it was limited by its geography. The residential location meant it had little room to expand, and there was not a great deal of space to develop other facilities which could provide the club with non-matchday income.

The board believed the club had outgrown its traditional home and set about identifying a site to build a new one as part of a project which would be supported by Coventry City Council.

That was the former gasworks site, in Holbrooks, and plans for a 40,000-seater stadium were soon drawn up by Coventry architect Geoff Mann. Billed Arena 2000, it included a retractable roof and a sliding pitch, with the aim of staging World Cup matches should England's bid to host the tournament in 2006 become successful.

In a glossy brochure produced to promote the plans, Bryan Richardson declared the development would 'make a national impact on sport and leisure'.

He added: 'We are clear this will be a venue vying for World Cup football, world championship boxing, tennis tournaments, hockey and equestrian events, as well as major concerts and exhibitions. We believe the project will provide the city with a landmark it can be proud of.

'It is essential we seek ways of increasing our current Highfield Road capacity, whilst at the same time increasing in a substantial way the income we receive to allow us to compete with bigger clubs.'

That same brochure also included comments from the then leader of Coventry City Council, John Fletcher, who waxed lyrical about the project he predicted could be a 'vital shot in the arm for the area'.

He added: 'The whole idea is spectacular. It has massive potential. We are very excited but must also ensure proper scrutiny of the proposals to make sure the right decisions are made for Coventry.'

Geoffrey Robinson said the entire board backed the project from the very beginning.

He said: 'It was very exciting. Bryan was a tremendous entrepreneur. The original idea was very risky from the beginning, but we all went along with it.

'It relied on a level of commitment and goodwill from the council that never really came to fruition.

'Both sides were to blame as it went along, but it did presuppose that it would be a successful development for the council and the club with goodwill, give and take all the way through.'

John McGuigan, then development chief for Coventry City Council, said the authority always saw the project as an opportunity to regenerate a downtrodden part of the city.

He said: 'For many years, the football club had been looking for a new ground. Highfield Road was a model of what a football ground should be, but the site was hugely restricted by location.

'About half the big home games they had, they were having to lock people out – when teams like Manchester United and Chelsea came to town.

'Their ability to grow non-football revenues was hugely limited.

'My understanding is they had looked at sites around Warwick University, around Ansty and some derelict sites in the north of the city. But none of them were big enough.

'The council in the 1990s had a clear idea that the city had to grow. We had a boom city that had hit bad times in the 1970s and it had taken all of 20 years to stabilise that.

'We had to put energy into the north of the city. People who came to Coventry off the M6 were greeted by a disused colliery and a derelict gasworks.

'For 30 years, there had been all sorts of things suggested for the gasworks site, but none of them were big enough to make it work.

'The Ricoh was the key to a project that aimed to regenerate both sites in the zone labelled the North Coventry Regeneration Zone.

'There wasn't a district centre in the north of the city and we were anxious to help the football club relocate from Highfield Road.'

He added: 'We made it very clear from the beginning we were not interested in replacing a football stadium with a football stadium.

'We wanted a venue that could host concerts and attract big business conferences. We wanted a landmark building that could change the image of the north of the city from that of a derelict gasworks.

'That's why the idea of bidding to host World Cup matches came up. To do that required a minimum capacity of 40,000.

'The design originally was two tier, the idea being there would be a huge curtain that would be drawn across the upper level when you didn't need the whole thing. But that was too big.

'A retractable roof and pitch allowed it to be turned into an exhibition hall.

'One hundred metres by 70 metres of grass stood in an 18in-deep concrete tray. It would have weighed about 12,000 tonnes and sat on Teflon pads.

'Six days a week, when it wasn't being used, it would have sat outside on the south of the ground so it could get the sunlight.

'There was going to be a train station under the car park.

'When Bryan Richardson showed us the plans, our initial reaction was, "you are joking?"

'There was only one other similar facility in the world, the Gelredome in Arnhem, Holland, which we went to visit.

'That was only a 20,000-seater stadium, but the idea of the Teflon pads was there.

'We always had misgivings about the idea because it was predominantly still a football stadium.

'If we were trying to bring a big exhibition to the city, we would not be sure if the venue would be available because the club could be playing a midweek game or a cup game. That meant the non-football income was in doubt.

'But if England had won its bid to host the World Cup, we would have gone for that.'

Speaking during an interview with the BBC in 2012, Bryan Richardson made it clear he felt the club had no option but to build a new stadium.

He said: 'It was the only chance we had.

'We averaged 19,000 a game and brought in receipts of £5m a year. Arsenal and Manchester United make that in one match now. Our break-even attendance at the time would have been 83,000.'

In 1998, the club successfully applied for planning permission to demolish Highfield Road and build a new stadium at the gasworks site. But, as costs for the mammoth project increased, the club's board decided to sell Highfield Road for around £4m in 1999 and lease the ground back.

This was a pivotal moment, and one which Geoffrey Robinson later described as 'a disastrous mistake'.

He said: 'We sold Highfield Road outright in order to do it.

'The whole thing, as it turned out with hindsight, was a disastrous mistake for the club. It needn't have been. The original deal was great.

'Looking back, I think we should have got to the point where we had the money before we sold Highfield Road.'

He added: 'We got a good price. It was the whole board's decision to sell.

'It was a big decision and a gamble that everybody decided to go for. Football was in one of its big upward swings.

'If you wanted to stay in the Premier League, you needed your own modern stadium.'

John McGuigan said: 'The football club put in a joint planning application for Highfield Road and the Arena at the same time in 1998.

'They had to be put in at the same time because if you were removing a sports facility you had to demonstrate it would be replaced, otherwise Sport England – the governing body at the time – could have vetoed the application.'

He added: 'The disposal of Highfield Road got about £3m to £4.5m for housing. But the bank took that straight from them.'

The scale of the project, and the chance for Coventry to host World Cup matches, may seem like pie-in-the-sky looking back, but it was a very real vision at the time – and one which attracted the attention of the football world.

John McGuigan added: 'The FIFA hosting committee visited us. I went down to London with Bryan for a big slap-up dinner.

'I was on the main table with Hugh Grant, Bryan and Kevin Keegan. There were 80 people at the dinner and the room was full of the big names in English football.

'It shows how much the design of the stadium had attracted attention.

'But England didn't win the World Cup [bid] and we had to revisit the whole issue of the design and how it would work.'

One year later, England's bid to host the 2006 World Cup failed and the wheels began to wobble on the new stadium project.

The plans had to be redrawn, the original designs were too expensive and did not offer enough potential for non-matchday revenue. They eventually moved towards the design we recognise as the Ricoh Arena today.

The club was in serious financial trouble not least because the Co-Op Bank, which had huge amounts of money invested with football clubs, had launched a drive to reduce its level of lending – including to Coventry City.

John McGuigan said: 'At the time the club was £60m in debt, including a £20m loan from Geoffrey Robinson.

'The Co-Op were the football club's bank, and at that time they had started a drive to lower the debts of all the football clubs on their books.'

Geoffrey Robinson has never confirmed exactly how much he committed to the club during his time on the board, but he did indicate it was tens of millions.

He said: 'I regret the costs obviously. But I have regrets in the sense that I didn't succeed. We let the fans down dreadfully.

'That's my overriding regret: we failed, we failed the club. We failed in our objectives to get the club to stay up and the finances straight – we didn't do either.

'It was a golden period when we got involved in the late 1990s. My first money went in in 1996. Nobody regrets the great times, the players, the fans above all.

'I made the money available far too easily in retrospect. I trusted people far more than I should have. But that's not central to the big issue.

'I put £10m in the club and we had Whelan, Kevin Richardson, Darren Huckerby – a group that kept us going for five or so years. We didn't quite make it, but they were great years. I don't regret those.'

The club had a preliminary agreement to buy the gasworks site from British Gas and Bryan Richardson recruited Dutch construction firm HBG to decontaminate the site ready for the new stadium to be built.

But catastrophe struck on 5 May 2001 – a day many Sky Blues fans will look back on as the single biggest moment in the club's post-war history. The club was relegated from the Premier League. With relegation came a dramatic drop in income. It marked a downturn in the club's fortunes which many will argue continues today.

But the biggest implication at the time was that Coventry City's financial troubles were severely worsened. This hugely undermined the club's ability to continue with the new stadium project. Reports at the time suggest the club suffered debts in the region of £60m, including bank loans and loans from board members.

Geoffrey Robinson said: 'We had failed. We always threw everything at staying up.

'You can't blame any of the club's debts on the stadium, I don't think. They were big already and the stadium didn't give us the lift we needed.

'To stay in the Premier League is a real big art. We gambled on staying up, and we failed.'

HBG came to the football club for payment as the final gas tower was demolished at the site in 2002, but there was a problem. The club had no money, and it transpired British Gas still owned the gasworks land as the club's preliminary deal to secure the site had never been formalised.

The Dutch construction firm went over the club's head to secure the land from British Gas, before convincing the council to purchase the 70 acres of land from them for £20m or risk losing the entire stadium project. That same weekend, the council sold the land to Tesco for £60m after Bryan Richardson had negotiated the deal with his personal friend and Tesco chief executive Sir Ian MacLaurin – a deal Bryan Richardson is understood to have collected a £1m bonus for.

John McGuigan said: 'HBG, a Dutch construction company, built the original stadium in Arnhem. They were really the only people we could trust to build this stadium.

'Bryan offered them the contract to build the stadium. Because the club was running the project at that stage, they didn't have to go through the sort of tender process the council would have.

'HBG came over and decontaminated the land. Then when they asked for payment, Bryan said, "we haven't got any money."

'HBG wanted to take a charge over the land, but then discovered the football club didn't own it and it was still owned by British Gas.

'When they found out the football club didn't own the land, HBG made a contract with British Gas to buy it all.

'They then said to the council, unless you step in and buy the land, the stadium is gone. They said they would proceed with a retail development.

'The council paid £20m for the site, which was 70 acres. We then sold 30 acres to Tesco for £60m. Both deals were done in the same weekend.

'The figure for buying the gasworks part of the site was only £2m. I understand Bryan awarded himself a £1m bonus for doing that part of the deal – but he never actually did it.

'If the council had not stepped in, it would not have happened. There were five or six occasions during the course of this project when the council had to step in. Sometimes it wasn't just about money.'

Shortly afterwards, Bryan Richardson was ousted in a boardroom coup by his fellow board members and Mike McGinnity took over as chairman. Richardson had gone, but his vision of a new home for the Sky Blues lived on.

Geoffrey Robinson said: 'The key thing was to ensure we got our 50 per cent of the Arena. But then Bryan fell out with the board and he went just as the plans were under way.

'The concept was clearing up a wretched part of Coventry, put a marvellous stadium there and, realising its value, bringing in Tesco – Bryan did all that, he was brilliant, and it was very good.'

In 2002, the club and the council formed Arena Coventry Limited (ACL) – the firm responsible for the Arena – in which they were equal partners.

By 2003, the club had invested an estimated £2m in the project, but they were now strapped for cash.

Through board member and Alan Edward Higgs Charity boss Derek Higgs, they applied for a loan to provide the £21m needed to complete the Arena project from Banco Espirito Santo.

But that loan ultimately fell through and the council, fearing its regeneration project for the north of the city might not be delivered, committed to lend £21m to Arena Coventry Limited (ACL).

John McGuigan said: 'We created a company called Coventry North Regeneration to build the Arena. It was an "arms length" company, which meant that if it went bust it would not have an impact on the council. But it could not take advantage of tax allowances.

'There was a figure of £21m for the fit-out of the stadium – and that became the loan we are still talking about today. We wanted ACL to take on the finance for that for tax purposes.

'The football club negotiated that loan with Banco Espirito Santo. But they said they would only do it if the council guaranteed the deal, and we would not do that.

'The loan fell through and we had to postpone the full council meeting to sign off the project for a month.

'Ultimately, the council agreed to put £10m in and we would give ACL a £21m loan.

'Soon after, Yorkshire Bank took over that £21m loan from the council.

'We always thought that, when that debt was cleared, ACL would make £4m a year.'

Geoffrey Robinson said the club's inability to secure finance for the project was a key moment leading up to the situation we have today, but also pointed the finger at the city council for failing to support the club.

He told me: 'Where it went wrong was when we couldn't come up with the money for the club's part, which was about £20m.

'Derek Higgs would have to carry the can for that. He was in charge of the negotiations with the bank. He failed.

'At that point, John McGuigan stepped in and said, "this will now be a council-led project."

'The idea of a joint-venture project went out the window. It would be run by the council and it was one disaster after another. I predicted to John McGuigan it would be. They're not set up to do that. It was a big failure from that point on.

'The council took on the loan and that became the now-infamous loan that is still being argued about today.

'We couldn't walk away when we failed to get the loan from the bank. We'd sold Highfield Road by then.'

He added: 'That £20m is where we failed. At that point, the council stepped in eagerly thinking they had got a bargain and thought "screw the club". That was their attitude, sadly. They were non-commercial and unrealistic.

'When the council stepped in with the loan, at the time we breathed a sigh of relief. We could have gone back to another bank to get the money and asked for a stay of execution. But the council was certainly the easiest option.

'You couldn't say the council were being overtly forceful in pushing through their solution, but I think they were very keen to do it.

'My judgement here is that the council saw this as their big moment. John McGuigan said to me, with an air of grandeur, "this will be a council-led project from now on." They had put the money up so you couldn't deny them that control.'

He added: 'We should have stayed at Highfield Road, no question about it, having failed in all the other objectives we set ourselves – to own and control the new stadium, to stay up and when we failed with the loan.'

Despite the project getting under way, the club's troubles were far from over. Under pressure to reduce their debts further, the club agreed a deal to sell their shares in ACL to the Alan Edward Higgs Charity for £6.5m.

The deal was only ever meant to be a short-term arrangement, and a formula was agreed for the club to buy back the shares in the future. In fact a 2003 council report, which formed the basis of the council agreeing to support the project, anticipated that the club would have bought back the shares and ACL would have cleared its bank debts within ten years.

Peter Knatchbull-Hugessen is clerk of the Higgs Charity and husband to Marilyn Knatchbull-Hugessen – chairman of the charity and sister of Derek Higgs. He explained how the charity had become involved with the deal.

He said: 'The charity was already heavily involved with the club when the ACL shares issue came up. The charity had loaned the club £2.5m secured against the value of players.

'The objective of the loan was essentially about remembering 1987. The loan was made in the early 1990s, when the 1987 FA Cup win and the effect it had was still in the trustees' minds. They wanted to continue that and so they set it up as a cash investment.

'It was done with proper legal advice and they paid instalments as you would with any other loan.

'When it came to the time that loan needed to be repaid, it was post-Bosman. We had a guarantee of double the loan in players, but after Bosman that was not as secure. The club could offer no security.

'We knew the club was in a parlous state, so we said you have to pay the money back.

'At the same time Geoffrey Robinson had loaned the club £5m, but our loan had to be paid back before his.

'The result was that they could not pay the money back. The charity was faced with forcing the club to go into administration. Clearly, we did not want that to happen.

'At the end of the 2002/03 season, they needed more money just to start the next season. They were not able to borrow any more because of all the other loans they had not paid back.

'At this time, ACL was just being set up. So we got the shares in ACL for £6.5m and they got £4m in cash and £2.5m was effectively paid back to the charity.

'The shares had a formula for the club to buy them back and the intention was it would be a short-term deal, although there was no official timeline.

'From the charity's perspective, it was lose £2.5m or do the deal.'

He added: 'The charity believed it was very important to secure the building of the Arena for Coventry. The north west of the city was a regeneration zone.

'There needed to be something that would create employment benefit, bring inward investment. Creating a relationship with the city council should have been a secure and sensible thing.

'We both had interests in the betterment of Coventry for the people. For the charity it was a two-way motive, a financial motive, and that it would benefit the people of Coventry.

'The deal was given the green light by Grant Thornton and legal advisers, who checked it over as a cash investment. We had to be sure it stacked up – and it did clearly, although it was deemed riskier than if we had invested in shares in a bank, for instance.

'We asked if it stacked up given the charity's objectives and the answer was yes it did.

'It was not about supporting the club.'

John McGuigan described the situation leading up to the sale of the club's shares in ACL from the council's perspective.

He said: 'One year into the project Stella Manzie, the council's chief executive, and I were summoned to Highfield Road.

'Bryan had gone by then and Mike McGinnity was in charge. He explained that the club was under severe pressure from the bank and had to sell its shares in ACL.

'I told Mike at the time "what you have sold is your income streams for the future."

'There were two options. Geoffrey Robinson could buy them or the Higgs Charity was prepared to buy them. He asked us who they should sell to.

'It took us all of ten seconds to decide it should be the charity.

'They were a regeneration charity, they didn't want to make a profit and they wanted to sell them back to the club eventually.

'Derek Higgs eventually did the deal. They ultimately put something like £6.5m in to buy the football club's 50 per cent share in ACL.

'The option agreement to buy back the shares in the future was something like 75 per cent of the 50 per cent at the original price and two per cent interest on the remaining 25 per cent.

'That was because, as a charity, they had to be seen to be getting recompense.'

Geoffrey Robinson acknowledged this was another area where the club's board had failed.

He said: 'We did a deal, which was Derek's idea again. It was another bad step.

'He failed on two things in this. But he was very good, and a wonderful chap. We must not speak badly of him.

'But there were two things he did that were utterly catastrophic from the point of view of the project.

'One was to fail to get the money we needed. We wouldn't have had a problem with it.

'In the wake of that, we then had a problem where, in addition to the £2m we put in, we had to find a further £4.5m.

'In hindsight, we should have dug into our pockets and put it back in.

'But the Higgs Charity put in their £6.5m and bought the club's half share in ACL off them.

'We were out of the project, but we had an option to re-buy it.

'The charity together with the council was an absolute disaster.'

The council committed £10m cash into the project and they worked with the football club to secure a further £10m in external funding.

After a lengthy and heated council meeting in October 2003, the local authority eventually signed off the deal and the Ricoh Arena project was officially under way.

Subsequently, the council agreed a deal with Yorkshire Bank to take over the ACL loan – the loan which ultimately became the subject of a lengthy legal battle between future owners Sisu and the city council.

John McGuigan gave an insight into why the council seemed resistant to signing off the deal at the time.

He said: 'The club put in about £2m to create the Arena 2000 company, get designs drawn up and secure planning permissions.

'The council said we would put £10m in and we would be 50/50 shareholders. The idea was that we would be back-seat passengers.

'In 2002, the company moved from Arena 200 to ACL. The council put in £10m and brought in £5m in European funding and another £5m from Advantage West Midlands.

'When we started construction, the football club owned half of ACL.

'They had essentially wasted £2m but hadn't put a penny more in.

'If the club was not there, the arena would not have been built. They added value that way. The council did want to help them. They still do, I've no doubt about that.

'It was nearly overturned on the day of the council, but that wasn't malicious. It was because Dave Nellist [a former Labour Coventry MP and Coventry City councillor at the time] put an amendment in.

'At the full council meeting where the stadium was agreed, Dave Nellist tabled a motion to vary the deal because the council had taken all the risk and put the most money in.

'I took Dave to one side and explained that for the integrity of the council and the deal, we had to proceed on the basis of 50/50. Without that, the deal would have collapsed.'

He added: 'The council never intended to run the scheme. We put £10m in to it as regeneration investment.

'We ended up in a situation where we were going to lose the whole site unless the council stepped up and took control of it.'

The subject of how much hard cash the club actually put into the project has been hotly debated in the past. Some of the club's historic accounts show wildly varying totals ranging between £6m and £11m being spent on the new stadium project.

But, according to the council's 2003 report ahead of the construction of the Arena being signed off, the club had contributed £2m. It reads: 'These resources have been used to meet the day-to-day office costs, legal and other specialist advice to ACL and elements of the initial phase of design work.'

That total also marries up with the council's Arena Construction Completion report, published in 2006, which puts the club's total financial contribution to the building of the £116m Ricoh Arena at £2m.

The council figures were also the ones subscribed to by Geoffrey Robinson when asked about how much the club had invested in the project – but he contested the club had added value in other ways

He said: 'Before we got there, three of us had to put a combined £2m seed fund in for the whole project.

'That was myself, Derek and Mike McGinnity. Without that money, the thing would never have got going.

'That was a cash donation to it. We did not get any money back, even when the Alan Edward Higgs Charity bought the club's half share in ACL.'

He added: 'The club itself didn't have any money to put into the project. There was the £2m which we put in.

'That would have been perhaps £1m or £2m in consultancy fees and so on, but hard cash – very little. There was £2m gift money from the three directors.

'You should argue that this money spent on architects and consultants was an investment by the club in the project.

'Having the idea is also a huge investment. Without that, you have nothing.'

He added: 'The club came out of it very badly in the end. For us to get 50 per cent of the project for nothing, our tenancy was what we were bringing. We had no other assets.

'We had £20m to find, and we failed. To get 50 per cent of everything, and all the revenues attached, for £20m would have been a fabulous deal for the club.

'But we brought the potential of revenue, we made the deal possible by offering the football club as the base stone for the profits for the whole stadium on an ongoing basis.

'We were going to get 50 per cent of the ground by offering nothing more than the club.

'It was a good deal for the club, and it was a fabulous deal for the council too. It would have been a good deal for everybody. That's the point of a good deal.'

Another point of contention soon arose over the level of rent and how it was set.

It would come back to haunt the club after the £1.3m annual rent fee ultimately led to a dispute which saw the club leave the Ricoh Arena and play home matches at Sixfields for more than a season.

John McGuigan explained how the rent level was calculated at the time.

He said: 'This was all based on the premise that it would be a Premier League team in a Premier League stadium. In that scenario, there would have been no problem at all.

'The way the Arena business was supposed to work was that they would pay around £1m in rent and they would be handed a cheque back for £2m.

'The rent had to be set at that level because we had to be careful about state aid law. We spent a fortune on European lawyers.

'With the club putting in £2m up front and getting planning permission, we could justify that deal. But for them to occupy and make use of the asset there had to be a rent.

'There was nothing similar to it anywhere in Europe that had already passed the test. There are quite a few council-owned grounds but they tended to be much smaller.

'We hired specialist companies [Pinsents, Renouf and LECG] who spent a lot of time on research.

'They said it would stand up to scrutiny if we charged them £1m a year in rent.

'My initial thoughts on that were that this is a bit of a surprise. I couldn't see huge evidence of why it was £1m.

'We then did basic research on the Highfield Road accounts. In previous years, they had spent about £800,000 running Highfield Road. Not on players or anything like that, purely on the running of the ground.

'Since they weren't going to be paying anything at the Arena, that made bigger sense.

He added: 'The whole Arena project came up at a cost of £113m. Of that, £64m was on the actual Arena. If you took the £64m Arena and stripped out the stadium bowl, that part would probably come out at about £25m.

'We then asked how much would the refinancing costs be if they built that stadium and it worked out at about £1.2m – that's how the rent figure was calculated.

'The advice we got was that the maximum lease we could offer was 45 years, maybe 50.

'In due course, you can extend that lease because the freeholder retains responsibility for the asset. In this instance we were not selling them the land, we were renting them the Arena. It was always intended that in due course we would restructure the lease and the club would take over all responsibility for running and managing the Arena.'

But it wasn't just the rent which was an issue. The licence deal ultimately hamstrung the club and saw the Sky Blues fail to get access to the very non-matchday revenues which had prompted the move away from Highfield Road in the first place.

Asked why the club agreed to pay a rent which seems astronomical in comparison to those paid by other football clubs which rent grounds, Geoffrey Robinson accepted the club's board was to blame. But he insisted, at that point, they had no choice, with the club already so far into the project and with no back-up option available.

He said: 'You have to point the finger at the club's board. But we didn't have any option, we were over a barrel – we'd sold Highfield Road.

'It wasn't just the rent deal, the revenue was just as bad – and not having control of development and being able to expand it. Any benefit of that went to ACL, not to the club.

'That's where it went wrong. We should have retained control of the Ricoh Arena.

'Paul Fletcher [then chief executive of ACL who went on to become managing director of the club] negotiated extraordinarily well for ACL, and the council. He did a good job – but it screwed the club. Everybody said at the time the rent wasn't affordable.

'We raised concerns at the time, all the way through. It wasn't just the rent, we gave away too much of the revenue.

'Paul negotiated for ACL, and Graham Hover [former club secretary] negotiated for us.

'We ended up paying too much rent and not getting enough of the revenue. We even gave away match day parking.'

He added: 'Even if we had halved the rent, it wouldn't have saved us. But about half a million would have been the right rent for it.

'We put all sorts of proposals forward – Premier League rent could have been higher, Championship rent would be lower – we said something like £400,000 to £500,000 – but that wouldn't have saved us. It might get you another season.

'Relegation was the breaking point for us, but even then Bryan Richardson was clinging on to the hope of an early return. But when we failed then, that was the end of it.

'We talked about tiered rent, at the time and afterwards, but they were all rejected by the council.'

Listening to the accounts of those directly involved, there is little doubt the club came out of negotiations very badly. But they went into them in a very weak bargaining position and no back-up plan. Fortune had also conspired against the people running the club, with relegation from the top flight coinciding with a drive from financial institutions to lower the level of debt acquired by football clubs. Looking back, do those involved feel they could have done anything differently to leave the club in a stronger position than it finds itself today?

Geoffrey Robinson said: 'I regret that we failed on the loan for the Ricoh Arena, that was a terrible failure. Selling our share in ACL and making the deal with the charity was the further mistake.

'But the huge mistake for everybody was the council coming in to run it.'

John McGuigan added: 'What would I have changed looking back? Lots and lots.

'But I have yet to meet anybody who says the Ricoh Arena is not good for Coventry.

'The one thing I would have done more than anything else was simplify it. It was such a complex scheme. But the council can't decide how commercial organisations like football clubs operate. Things happen in a commercial environment that you don't expect.

'If the football club had got back into the Premier League, the entire saga of the past five years would not have happened.'

Chapter Two

Hello Ricoh Arena

THE date of 30 April 2005 is of huge significance to Coventry City fans. This was the day that the Sky Blues bid an emotional farewell to the club's home of 106 years.

For anyone lucky enough to get into Highfield Road that day, it is an occasion none of us will ever forget.

The atmosphere was one of sadness, but also one of hope and expectation. Hope that the Ricoh Arena, which had revealed its naming rights sponsor just days before, would provide the launchpad needed for Coventry City to become a real force in English football. Perhaps that air of sadness would have been heightened had fans known what cruel tests the future actually had in store.

The last game at Highfield Road was an almost perfect occasion. Players from bygone years were paraded on the sun-drenched pitch before the match, but it was the class of 2004/05 who ensured the club bowed out in style.

A fired-up Coventry team, including local youngsters Gary McSheffrey and Marcus Hall, demolished a shell-shocked Derby County side, killing off the game as a contest by half time when the Sky Blues went in leading by four goals.

A 6-2 victory was capped off when academy product Andrew Whing hammered in a spectacular goal, which was no less than the spiritual home of Coventry City deserved as a sign-off.

Cue the Mexican wave, as the club's unofficial anthem *Twist and Shout* rang out around the ground ahead of the final whistle. Then came the pitch invasion as the referee signalled the end of the game.

It was a truly magical end to the life of a once cutting-edge stadium that had been bursting at the seams, with over 51,000 supporters on the club's way to the top flight where – for 34 proud years – great players from George Best to David Beckham had graced the hallowed turf.

But as the celebrations eased, manager Micky Adams addressed the crowds on the pitch from the main stand. He added to the hope and expectation by insisting that avoiding relegation in the Championship was not good enough for a club like Coventry City. He was right, of course, but little did he know the scale of the turbulent times which lay ahead. Few could have foreseen that the Sky Blues would end up in their current predicament while filled with optimism on that glorious spring day.

After Adams had finished his crowd-pleasing speech, there really was only one man who could wave Highfield Road off in the way it deserved – Coventry's most successful manager of all time, the man who had led the Sky Blue revolution from that very stadium in the 1960s; Jimmy Hill.

As he led the crowd in a rendition of the Sky Blue Song, there were tears. Tears of sadness as the club bid farewell to Highfield Road, but also tears of joy as people reminisced about the good times, the memories and the history which had been created in the stadium.

But now it was time to make new memories in the large new arena constructed to accommodate the football club's big ambitions. However, it was not quite the smooth transition those involved would have hoped for. A superstitious person might even suggest the project was cursed from the beginning, with the amount of hurdles which had to be overcome. Some of the problems remain until this day.

Many people will know that the new Arena was originally meant to be sponsored by Jaguar, a prestigious and fitting sponsor in many people's eyes bearing in mind the luxury car manufacturer's strong Coventry roots.

But it's no secret that around this time the car firm hit a major speed bump, with the company getting into financial difficulty and the Browns Lane manufacturing plant being shut down.

That meant the impressive artists' impressions circulated in the months before the Arena's completion – featuring a gigantic Jaguar leaping from the Arena's roof – never became reality. It also meant wasted time, effort and money put into strengthening the roof of the Arena so that it could support the giant Jaguar sculpture.

John McGuigan explained that the council and ACL had essentially let Jaguar off the hook. Despite the firm's cold feet, the deal had already been signed and sealed and was legally binding.

He said: 'It's probably well known that it was going to be the Jaguar Arena. Naming rights and sponsorship was always seen as an important element of ACL's funding – for example The E.on Lounge, Yorkshire Bank Lounge, stand naming etc.

'The whole Arena was going to be called the Jaguar Arena and we had to strengthen the structural design and roofing of the egg-shaped façade to the building that fronts on to the A444/Rowleys Green roundabout to enable the structure to be able to take the planned huge leaping cat.

'The deal had been signed but we understand when Ford, Jaguar's then parent company in the USA, heard about this they got upset because of Jaguar's difficult financial position.

'For obvious reasons we didn't want to proceed with the naming rights contract, even though it was signed and legal, when Jaguar management was in some difficulty.'

But the failure to sign off on the naming rights deal was actually a huge stroke of luck for the Ricoh Arena business in financial terms.

Jaguar had promised £5m for the naming rights, but stadium bosses eventually secured a deal for double that.

Just days before Coventry played their last game at Highfield Road, the eventual naming rights sponsor was announced. It came in the shape of Japanese copier firm Ricoh – perhaps not quite as prestigious as the original plans – but it did provide a valuable £10m boost to ACL's coffers.

Coventrians do seem to get everywhere, so it's perhaps little surprise that the naming rights deal came about, in part, as a result of a Coventry connection within the firm.

John McGuigan explained: 'The Ricoh company which operated in Britain and across the world under many different brand names was looking to consolidate their name/brand, especially in terms of their UK business.

'One of their senior managers in their UK business was a Coventry kid and an avid CCFC supporter.

'He used to periodically take his boss to games at Highfield Road. His boss constantly and in jest would deride CCFC because of the state of Highfield Road.

'After one such game, and just as the huge superstructure of the new Arena was being built on the old gasworks site, he drove his boss up to the site and said, "So this is the club without any ambition, is it?"

'That visit, the Arena's location and profile etc all quickly generated interest from Ricoh UK.

'Therefore Ricoh stepped in as main naming sponsor, with smaller Jaguar sponsorship of the exhibition hall.

'ACL actually got double what it would have got from the original Jaguar contract. So it was a win-win all round.'

Now we knew what the Arena would be called, but the problems were far from over.

There were fears the Arena would not be ready in time for the start of the 2005/06 season – fears which necessitated extra money to be thrown at the project in order to avoid serious embarrassment.

Arena construction firm Laing O'Rourke informed the council that construction was three months behind schedule.

With Highfield Road already sold and the process of dismantling the stadium under way, serious action had to be taken.

So ,as parts of Highfield Road were being auctioned off as memorabilia, the council agreed to inject an extra £2m into the project in order to reduce the three-month delay to three weeks.

That took the total spend for the contract with Laing O'Rourke up to £57m, according to the council's Ricoh Arena Completion Report of June 2006. That was £2.7m over the original budget.

There was also a £2.6m overspend on the 'fit-out' of the stadium, taking those costs up to £7m. That overspend was partly blamed on the cost of the £250,000 scoreboard, a £150,000 telephone system and £800,000 spent fitting out the on-site leisure centre.

The extra fit-out costs were split between the council and ACL, who supplied £1.1m via extra financial support from Yorkshire Bank with the council picking up the remaining £1.5m tab.

The three-week delay to the project meant that Coventry had to play their first three matches of the season away from home. But even that almost wasn't enough, with the safety certificate for the stadium only signed off on the morning of the club's first home game against QPR.

There were also countless other issues which rumbled on behind the scenes for months after Coventry's first game, but the Sky Blues were at least in their new home.

John McGuigan said: 'As the start of the football season loomed, Laing O'Rourke announced that completion would be at least three months delayed – citing issues with [sub-contractor] Haden Young.

'It could be accelerated to a three-week delay, but we'd have to pay them £2m to fund this acceleration.

'For obvious reasons, this is something I had to do and argue the case afterwards. With Sir Derek Higgs' help, we got two meetings with Ray O'Rourke, the owner of Laing O'Rourke, still a privately-owned company.

'Despite our arguments and our implied threats to chastise them publicly and advise other public bodies not to tender to them, Ray O'Rourke continued to argue his corner.

'But the £2m we ultimately paid was significantly less than Laing O'Rourke originally wanted.

'In reality, whilst CCFC had to play away for the first three weeks of the new season, the final completion of the Arena – particularly its complex fit-out and finishes and dealing with all the snagging works identified – took another six months, but little of this would have been apparent to the general public.

'Notwithstanding all this, in hindsight Laing O'Rourke weren't a bad company to deal with. Their project director on the job was good, as were his senior management.

'It seems that the Ricoh Arena scheme unfortunately got caught up in the bigger issues that Laing O'Rourke was dealing with at that time, issues that we didn't know about.

'As but one example of practical problems we encountered when finally opening the Ricoh, we had to operate a summer menu in all our corporate catering facilities for at least the first six weeks after opening day because – between Laing O'Rourke and Haden Young – they'd installed the wrong size gas governor for the whole building, and we could only operate with our electric ovens until the correct gas governor was procured and installed and the main gas supply and the big gas ovens could be switched on.'

Coventry City's first game at the Ricoh Arena was held on 20 August 2005, and it was a day to remember.

Unfortunately, safety restrictions prevented the 32,609-seater stadium from being filled to capacity. But the 23,012 people who were able to get a ticket for the opening game were treated to a feisty 3-0 victory over Queens Park Rangers.

The game had an added edge, with Coventry players and management unhappy with the way QPR had celebrated beating City in an ill-tempered final of a pre-season tournament in Ibiza.

But it was the Sky Blues who had the last laugh, cruising to an impressive victory as they christened the Ricoh Arena in style.

Nobody summed up the occasion better than former *Coventry Telegraph* sports editor Rob Madill. His report read: 'The sound of *In our Coventry home* was ringing around the Ricoh Arena.

'It was 3.05pm on Saturday 20 August 2005 and the Sky Blue faithful were settling into their new stadium by singing an old anthem.

'It had been a difficult, stressful move. With no money to buy, City had to rent, delays had put the completion date back and the property still wasn't quite finished.

'Doubts had been expressed about the wisdom of selling a perfectly good property to be tenants in a flashier more expensive new one.

'Yet five minutes later the agonies had turned to ecstasy, Claus Jorgensen headed in and the Ricoh rocked for the very first time.

'The roar was deafening, 23,000 voices exploding with joy, relief and the knowledge that all the anxieties were over – this truly was the Sky Blues' new home.

'And what a home. A mass of steel and concrete welded into a stunning structure. Sweeping stands, wonderful views, a superb setting for football. A field of dreams surrounded by a sea of Sky Blue.

'Even at only three-quarters full, the noise was amazing. Passion poured on to the pitch from the massed ranks of the Sky Blue Army – the West End and the Kop joined together in the new Coventry Evening Telegraph stand to create a formidable new force that, on this evidence, can be worth a goal start to the team.

'Dele Adebola made it 2-0 and the roars were so loud they must have been heard in Highfield Road – you remember, that place where City used to play, and now almost forgotten amid the awe-inspiring magnificence of the Ricoh.

'Twenty minutes later it was 3-0. "Easy, easy" chanted the fans, the game now almost becoming incidental to the occasion. The house-warming party was in full swing and the gracious visitors from Queens Park Rangers had no intention of spoiling it. It was heady stuff.

'Like any good party, after the intoxication comes the singing. In the second half, the Sky Blue Song reverberated around the ground in celebration and pride.

'Jimmy Hill had been brought on to sing his Coventry City anthem before the game, a reminder of that memorable last day at Highfield Road last April and a piece of symbolism to create a little of the old ground's atmosphere at the new one.

'It was scarcely needed. As the game ended the manager responded to cries of "Micky, Micky, give us a wave" with a raised hand of acknowledgement. Even with Hill's vision, the man who created the first all-seater stadium in England at Highfield Road in 1981 could surely never have envisaged his beloved Sky Blues playing in such a venue as this.

'As the Sky Blues supporters trooped out, delighted with their team's win and even more delighted with their new surroundings, it was somehow fitting that the concourses and staircases they walked down, and the bars and the toilets they had used, weren't quite finished.

'They know that, like their team, there's much work to be done before they can sit back and admire the view.

'But for now, they'll take the three points and the knowledge that their team plays in one of the best grounds in the country.'

Coventry manager Micky Adams was also impressed, although he clearly hadn't been completely won over by the time of the post-match press conference.

He said: 'The stadium was terrific and the fans made a tremendous noise, which gave the players the confidence to go out and play.

'There are certain things that need to be addressed but I'm sure they will be. This is a fantastic stadium and I'm sure that in two or three weeks time all the faults will have been ironed out.'

But despite the excitement, there was a suggestion the club had not made the most of this move and the opportunity it presented.

There were the obvious issues with the sale of the club's share in the operating company, but many felt the club had failed to capitalise on the opportunity to attract a new generation of fans to the club and boost attendances in a way that many had hoped for prior to the move.

John McGuigan said: 'Notwithstanding their deep involvement right from the beginning and their continued input even when they no longer owned the ACL shares, CCFC never really seemed to understand the scope, scale and opportunities that the Ricoh gave them.

'Even a few weeks before the first game at the Ricoh, CCFC directors and senior officials were being shown round the building as the carpets were being laid and equipment moved in.

'I remember being told by several of them as we walked round the corporate facilities, bars and conference and catering areas in the West Stand "I didn't know it would be so big."

'Upon polite questioning from me, it was quickly and surprisingly clear that they'd done very little to increase their season ticket sales, corporate hospitality engagement with the business community in the city etc.

'CCFC seemed, in some ways, to be in awe of the building rather than understanding and maximising their commercial opportunities from it.

'Evidence elsewhere had shown that, on average, new stadiums had delivered a 40 per cent increase in season ticket sales in their first year, but I don't believe CCFC went anywhere near this.

'Without exonerating CCFC from ineffective commercial management, it always seemed to me that, throughout this process, CCFC directors and senior management were constantly fire-fighting the impact and consequences of their dire financial situation, which had little or nothing to do with the Ricoh, ACL or the council.'

The Higgs Charity's Peter Knatchbull-Hugessen, also a director of ACL at this time, was also critical of the approach of the football club. He suggested animosity from the football club had played a part in a less-than-perfect working relationship. He said it had been strained after then-Coventry chairman Mike McGinnity saw his stadium seating company Pell miss out on the contract to fit out the Ricoh Arena.

Peter Knatchbull-Hugessen told me: 'McGinnity was invited to sit on the board of ACL but they did absolutely nothing towards the promotion of the place. All the offers to get signage installed, they refused.

'As soon as McGinnity found out he could not get Pell seats installed at the stadium, he became apathetic and uncooperative.

'But he also made some absolutely mad spending decisions. He wanted ACL to spend £100,000 redecorating the brand new boardroom suite that had just been decorated, which we refused.

'They spent thousands installing wood panelling in the brand new changing rooms, which had perfectly good tiling. Strange decisions like that were not uncommon.'

He added: 'The relationship was broken under McGinnity, it was dysfunctional. [It included] swearing in board meetings because they had not bought his more expensive seats.

'He used to say that ACL were only interested in ripping off the football club. He couldn't see that ACL directors had to act in the best interests of the business.

'We were already fighting them to get rent.'

But to fans, largely shielded from the financial troubles faced by the club, the move to the Ricoh Arena was the dawn of a new era.

The 2005/06 season was the beginning of *Operation Premiership*, an initiative launched by Paul Fletcher, club marketing director Ken Sharp and the club's finance chief Mal Brannigan.

It aimed to capitalise on the new-found enthusiasm surrounding the club following the move to the Ricoh Arena and it had a seemingly simple objective – a return to the top flight of English football within three years.

While no doubt launched with good intentions, today the campaign has become something the club's fans view with derision and point to as just another farcical moment in the long-term decline of their beloved Sky Blues.

Chapter Three

Sisu the saviours

C OVENTRY City had not long been at the Ricoh Arena when the weight of the financial difficulties facing them finally threatened to break the club's back.

Chairman Mike McGinnity had battled desperately to balance the books in a bid to keep the Sky Blues from going under. He is widely credited with reducing the club's debts from a reported figure of £60m to a more manageable £25m.

But that fight had clearly taken its toll on the then 64-year-old and, in November 2005, McGinnity made the decision to stand down as chairman.

He later took up the honorary role of life president while Coventry North West MP and long-serving club board member Geoffrey Robinson stepped into his shoes.

Tensions continued to increase at the brand-spanking new stadium as cracks began to appear in the relationship between the club and their Ricoh Arena landlords.

A seemingly petty dispute over the erection of a club crest sign threatened to boil over after the club's managing director, Paul Fletcher, gave the order to slap a five-metre tall badge on the side of the stadium. The stadium freehold was owned by the council, but the sign was erected without first seeking the permission of the local authority or their partners in Ricoh Arena operating firm ACL – the Higgs Charity.

The rebellious act was a clever PR move by the club's managing director, who clearly wanted to send the message that the Ricoh Arena was Coventry City's stadium, regardless of who was running it or who owned the bricks and mortar.

But both sides made the right noises in public as they aimed to brush the incident under the carpet.

Speaking at the time, Coventry City Council's John McGuigan told the *Coventry Telegraph*: 'It is not a problem to us.

'The sign is in the right place and is the sort of proposition that we would have supported anyway, but we are annoyed that we haven't been asked.

'We have a commitment from the football club that no more signage goes up at the Ricoh without discussion with us.'

Paul Fletcher told the newspaper he was simply meeting supporters' demands for the badge to be erected.

He said: 'I have given the council my assurance that we won't be putting up any further signage without speaking to them.

'I am delighted that the council have taken this view and I would not have taken this risk had I thought it would cause them any embarrassment.'

With trouble also brewing in the club accounts, the board was looking for someone to buy the club. In mid-2007, it looked like there might be a new investor on the horizon. It came in the shape of consortium The Manhattan Group, which had been introduced to the club by then managing director Paul Fletcher.

Manhattan was led by Coventry schoolboy and Sky Blues fan Gary Hopkins. The sports business consultant first became interested when he visited the Ricoh Arena on behalf of US soccer team DC United who planned to use it as a model for their own new stadium. The consortium also included US investment bankers Sean D McDevitt and Philip B Harris, as well as investment advisor and attorney Roger Marment.

But, by October 2007, that deal had all but fallen apart. Interest rates in the US and changing business interests were publicly blamed. However, it is understood the buyers first became interested because they were under the impression they would be able to buy the club, ACL and the freehold of the Ricoh Arena as part of the deal – an offer which was never on the table and which ultimately led to the withdrawal of the bid.

That withdrawal didn't just signal the end of the road for Manhattan. Paul Fletcher resigned from his position as managing director of Coventry City soon afterwards and Geoffrey Robinson stepped down as chairman. Fletcher signalled his apparent weariness at trying to bring all parties together and get a deal done, while Robinson suggested he needed to channel his time into his parliamentary duties.

It was the end of Operation Premiership.

One man who wasn't too disappointed to see the back of Fletcher and Robinson was ACL director Peter Knatchbull-Hugessen.

He told me: 'Under Geoffrey Robinson, Paul Fletcher put together a business plan for the club in 2005 and it simply didn't make sense.

'It predicted the gate for the first game at the Ricoh would be 22 per cent higher than the average attendance at Highfield Road and would remain there. They didn't do the necessary marketing. They refused to get involved in it.

'Then there was the private seat licences [which gave supporters a padded seat and a name plate on their chosen seat at the stadium]. The sales were predicted to be double the number of season tickets that had ever been sold at Highfield Road. They were predicting better figures than Glasgow Rangers had got. The numbers were just bonkers.

'They were expecting gates that had never been achieved.

'I was told, under Robinson, some of the board were on bonuses relating to turnover, which meant the club didn't need to make money for them to get paid. It meant they could throw money at something and it didn't matter if it didn't make money, they'd still get their bonuses.

'I'd never heard of bonuses being paid on turnover before, but Robinson was happy with it.'

The departure of Robinson left board member Joe Elliott to fill the chairman's position and try to pull the club out of its catastrophic nosedive.

Joe Elliott had been involved closely with the club from a young age after growing up with tennis friends Peter Robins and Roger Mead. Peter was the son of former club chairman Derrick Robins and Roger was the son of Phil Mead, the former vice-chairman.

He joined the Vice Presidents Club in 1984 and was made an associate director by then chairman Bryan Richardson in 1993. After several years working closely with Mike McGinnity on the marketing and PR of the club, he was brought on to the main board in 2003.

He said: 'It was a decision of the heart and, as a businessman, I should probably have said no.

'The club was in a mess; it had no money and it had been relegated. There was a new stadium on the way but we were beginning to lose control of that. It was a turbulent time to join the board.

'I was able to bring in some serious money from sponsors. My own company put in £1m-plus and spent many years as sponsor of the youth team and half a season sponsoring the first team.'

Having been involved with the club at the time the problems began to emerge, Elliott was in a good position to understand what had gone wrong over the past decade – and what had led the club to the brink in late 2007.

He said: 'The club through the 1990s had spent too much money. The club ran up tens of millions in debt. There was no doubt they were aiming to win the Premier League and with hopes of European football.

'There was no money to do anything when I arrived on the board. Bryan Richardson had gone and Mike was doing his best to try and manage the terrible financial situation in the best way he could.

'The main priority was keeping the football club afloat. Issues to do with the Ricoh Arena had already gone by then. We were in a situation where the Higgs Charity had taken the club's half share and the council had stepped in.

'There were no discussions over the rent to start with. We were not in a good bargaining position.

'There were discussions after we had been there for a while. Had the club been in a position of any sort of strength, we might have been able to negotiate a reduction.

'Things became worse when Mike had to stand down due to health reasons and then Geoffrey took over for a time before it was left to me to take over as chairman.'

Peter Knatchbull-Hugessen confirmed the view that the rent was seemingly not a priority for successive chairmen despite the fact the club was struggling to pay it.

He said: 'No discussions were had about the shares in the early years. They didn't have the money and they had problems paying the rent.

'ACL had numerous discussions with them over the level of rent. Derek Higgs had suggested a scheme which would have seen the rent tiered according to gate and according to league position. In the Premier League, it would have been higher, further down the leagues lower.

'But McGinnity and Robinson rejected it out of hand.'

Asked to reflect on the situation towards the end of his board's reign, Geoffrey Robinson said he felt the club was close to returning to the top flight and putting their troubles behind them. But it wasn't to be, and one final throw of the dice under Iain Dowie failed to put the club on a course to battle its way up and out of the Championship.

He said: 'We did throw money at it, we threw effort at it. I thought we had a real chance of getting back with our last manager, Iain Dowie. But then he was hit by a lawsuit from Simon Jordan [the then-Crystal Palace chairman who had previously employed Iain Dowie] and that knocked him off his stride.

'That was the whole season gone.'

At the end of 2007, with the Sky Blues facing a seemingly insurmountable level of debt and the most likely buyer now out of the picture, it looked as though Coventry City faced the very real prospect of going into administration – and possibly out of existence.

But buyers did emerge, with Mayfair-based hedge fund Sisu becoming the eventual owners, and former Manchester City defender-turned-businessman Ray Ranson put forward as the football brains behind the bid.

How close the club actually were to administration has never been clear, but Joe Elliott famously said they were '20 minutes away' when the deal to sell to Sisu Capital was finally stuck.

He added: 'I wouldn't say we were ever on the edge before 2007, when it was critical.

'Mike had done a good job trying to save the club money, Geoffrey Robinson had invested an awful lot of money and quite rightly wanted to be less committed to the monetary feeding of the club.

'The Co-Op Bank were getting more concerned by the day.

'The club were very close to going into administration. It really was a case of the clock was ticking on the day the Sisu deal was agreed.

'The bank had been very patient and it was either the deal was done then or we would have gone into administration.'

Interestingly, Sisu wasn't the only show in town as the board stepped up its search for a bidder. Just how many organisations were sniffing around, who they were and how serious their interest could be considered varies depending on who you speak to.

But from talking to many of the key players involved in the talks it seems safe to say there were at least three, and maybe four, seriously interested parties at the end of 2007.

The Manhattan Group was no longer in the picture, but another potential investor had emerged in the shape of an unknown insurance businessman – although his interest later faded.

There was another organisation called Shapiro, an American disaster management organisation which operated across the globe – a perfect fit, some Sky Blues fans might say, with the club spending decades lurching from one crisis to another.

Finally, there was a group of investors called The Windsor Group, who had been brought to the table by Geoffrey Robinson.

But between the disappearance of the Manhattan Group and the emergence of more serious offers, the club's plight attracted a wide range colourful characters as potential suitors.

Peter Knatchbull-Hugessen revealed: 'There was a couple of Texans who had the hats, the boots, the belts – the full gear. They turned up shortly after Manhattan.

'But they turned around and got back on a plane after one meeting in the boardroom, never to be seen again.

'There was a scrap dealer from Essex who was interested.

'But as soon as they understood the size of the thing, and that it was not owned by the football club, they were gone in an instant – without exception.'

Joe Elliott said: 'The Manhattan Group was led by Gary Hopkins, who is a Coventry kid. He was a good guy and a friend of Daniel Gidney [then chief executive of ACL], but that one never happened.

'Shapiro were very pleasant to deal with and they worked on the deal for quite a time, but ultimately that fell through.

'That left Sisu, who were the last man, or woman, standing.

'Sisu, for one reason or another, were the only ones who stuck. They were very enthusiastic. I started speaking to Ray

Ranson, who convinced me he was the right man for the job of running the football club, and Sisu seemed to have a very solid business set up.

'They put a lot of time and effort into buying the club.'

Peter Knatchbull-Hugessen also gave me his view on the Manhattan Group. He said: 'I think Paul Fletcher was on a percentage if he could do a deal with The Manhattan Group.

'But they were a group that never provided proper proof of funding.

'We, as ACL, could not go any further because they never showed us they had any money. They talked about what they had been doing in Washington, but it didn't stack up.

'Robinson was also talking them up, because he would have rescued some of his money.'

Geoffrey Robinson has never publicly confirmed who his buyers were, but sources have confirmed that The Windsor Group was headed up by former Deloitte partner Stephen Ives. Ives had been struck off by the Institute of Chartered Accountants for fraud after an incident relating to a car purchase in March 1996.

But Geoffrey Robinson was keen to proceed with the deal as it was the one which would have given him the greatest return and limited his personal losses after ploughing money into the club over the previous decade.

He said: 'I had two buyers lined up – but John McGuigan blocked the move, suggesting he didn't think one of the people involved was fit and proper.

'They would have paid me off my guarantee, which was about £10m. I've lost more than £20m in the club.

'He had a very good footballing man with him. They had £25m ready to invest on top of buying me out for £10m. They knew who they wanted to buy and everything.

'Derek Higgs and Mike McGinnity had met him and agreed it was a good alternative. We met him in the House of Commons.

'We agreed it wasn't very clever what he did, but there was no crime.

'But John McGuigan would not allow the sale. The council had the right of veto over who we could sell to.'

'There was a requirement that the council had to endorse whoever the shares went back to.

'When Sisu came in, there were about six bids.

'One or two of the interested parties were simply interested in securing the Arena and said they'd find someone to run the football club, so they were quickly put aside.

'Others, we were told, had a chequered history and were or had been interested in taking over other football clubs.

'One group had tried to buy Nottingham Forest but most of the companies were not interested in the football club, they were interested in the property.

'Another was a disaster management company with a big presence in Europe.

'Sisu were the best of the bunch. Joe Elliott sweated blood to help Sisu take over.

'They said they intended to get the club promoted and that's how they would make money. They said 'we find distressed companies, turn them around and then sell them on.'

'They said 'we haven't got a football club but we have got about ten other companies.' I said we needed someone who knows about football to run the club so then they turned up with Ray Ranson.

'He was like a breath of fresh air.'

Peter Knatchbull-Hugessen confirmed he agreed with the decision to reject the Windsor Group's approaches, but said he was disappointed the Shapiro bid never got out of the starting gate.

He said: 'We told the Windsor Group we need proof of funding and Geoffrey said we would get it.

'We were told it was with the Co-Op bank. But Kroll, the club's financial advisers, who had been put there by the Co-Op to manage the club's finances, put us in contact with someone at the Co-Op, who said they didn't even have an account with them – and at one point had actually been refused one.

'Shapiro was a big US firm with an office in Stoke-on-Trent. They would have been a good possibility from what we saw of them, and much more real than a hedge fund.

'But they made the decision to walk away. They wanted the Ricoh for nothing, but neither the council nor the charity could give it away for nothing.'

Sisu were the only game in town and, during conversations with those directly involved in the football club's takeover, it became apparent that there were some early reservations over the sale of Coventry City to the hedge fund.

Geoffrey Robinson said: 'Ray was quite a good bloke from what I could tell, a good chairman.

'But Sisu was not my choice. I doubted their financial strength, I doubted their commitment.

'They were known to be distress buyers. I get on OK with Joy Seppala [chief executive of Sisu], but distressed purchases is what they specialise in. She picks things up for a song, does something with it and sells it on.

'With that background, how could I think it was great?'

But there seems to be little doubt that Sisu, at that time, presented the best opportunity to secure the future of the football club in the eyes of most involved. John McGuigan explained that Sisu's chief executive, Joy Seppala, left the entire takeover process in the hands of her trusted employee Onye Igwe – or Onyechinaeduanaghaefuuzo Nnatuwereugo Igwe to give him his full name. The Swiss-educated Nigerian would go on to be Sisu's main representative on the board for the next four years.

But before the council gave the deal their blessing, John McGuigan said he had pushed Sisu on their business plan and had impressed on them the level of funding required to turn the club around.

He also seemed to have some sympathy for Sisu, suggesting they had taken on more than they had bargained for.

Conversations with various parties have suggested the new owners were somewhat surprised to learn, after the deal had been completed, that there was a £5.5m tax bill which needed to be paid almost immediately.

John McGuigan said: 'When we first met Sisu, Onye Igwe was leading. Throughout all my time involved with ACL and the Ricoh, I've never met or had any dealings with Joy Seppala.

'My simple and fundamental question to Onye was 'why does a hedge fund/venture capitalist want to buy a lower division football team which is in severe financial difficulties?'

'Onye stated that Sisu's objective was to buy companies in difficulty, turn them round and then sell on. Their strength was in the turnaround process and in being able to bring significant new money into the equation.

'The deal between us, if they were the successful bidder for the club, was 'we've delivered a Premiership facility; you deliver us a Premiership team, since without that you'll never make any real money in the football business.'

'That remained the unwritten understanding as the discussions progressed. I also helped CCFC by demonstrating to Sisu that their initial promise of at least £5m working capital for the club was hopelessly undercooked.

'They really needed to have at least £20m up front to deal with the inherited problems and liabilities of CCFC that must be paid if they were to avoid administration and losing the Football League golden share [which grants teams the right to compete in the Football League].

'They ultimately accepted this and, notwithstanding what they said was significant due diligence work, I think they found more problems when they took over CCFC than they had anticipated.'

The issue of a share in the stadium to accompany the deal for the club was evidently raised prior to Sisu completing the deal for the Sky Blues. Peter Knatchbull-Hugessen also said he had warned Sisu in advance of the takeover of the club that the stadium issue might not be as straightforward as they had anticipated, following a change of leadership at Coventry City Council after a long battle in the public arena to get the project delivered.

He said: 'The charity had a separate meeting from the council with Sisu. Onye was with Laura Deering and Walter Bosco from Sisu, who were obviously very bright. But Onye didn't listen.

'He said we're going to do this and that with the stadium and I said 'it won't work like that.'

'The place had only just opened under Coventry City Council Conservative leader Ken Taylor, and now Labour had just got back in. There was no way the council, who had taken all the sticks and stones for getting it through, were not going to enjoy it for a while.

'I said the most important people for you to make friends with are the city council because they are really pleased with it at the moment.

'They were talking about taking the whole of ACL. People say it's not for a football club to develop a site, but it is if you want to be bigger and better than other football clubs.

'If you don't have revenue for 365 days a year, you aren't going to cut it.'

Geoffrey Robinson also said that Sisu had even made an initial payment with a view to securing a share in the stadium for £4.5m.

He said: 'They did have an interest in taking over ACL at the time because they paid £1m for the option to buy back the charity's share in the company.

'They thought they were getting it at a snip. They thought they would get 50 per cent of that stadium for £4.5m – that's a fabulous deal. That's what they bought into.

'It's not a fabulous deal if you just own a football club that's losing money.'

It's unclear what Sisu's view on the situation was at the time, but incoming chairman Ray Ranson did confirm that

Sisu had an option to pick up a share in the stadium soon after the takeover was announced.

His predecessor as club chairman, Joe Elliott, also said he was left under the impression that a deal for a share in ACL was all but agreed prior to the hedge fund completing the takeover of the club.

Peter Knatchbull-Hugessen confirmed a meeting with all the key players was held shortly before the football club's takeover to discuss the stadium issue.

He said: 'There was no timeline. There was an arrangement in principle that they could take over the charity's shares in ACL by exercising the option.

'The council shares were always considered a second step. Anybody who came along was always told the charity would go out first and then the council.

'The council wanted to make sure it wasn't asset stripped. We wanted to ensure its future.'

Joe Elliott also recalled the meeting. He said: 'I was called to a meeting, not long after we had been in touch with Sisu, with Mal Brannigan [club finance director at the time]. It was quite late one evening, I had been at the club 18 hours a day trying to keep everything running.

'Mal and I were in the office pouring over figures and issues the club had when we got a call from Daniel Gidney [ACL chief executive], who asked us if we could come up to the executive room at the Ricoh.

'In that room was John McGuigan [then development chief for Coventry City Council], Peter Knatchbull-Hugessen [Higgs Charity clerk], Daniel Gidney, Onye Igwe [Sisu Capital] and Laura Deering [Sisu Capital].

'They said the stadium was a big issue and of interest to the football club and Sisu.

'They said they had agreed Sisu would be able to buy the half share in ACL from the Higgs Charity if they buy the football club, so go on and see if you can get the deal for the football club over the line.

'The fact they came in and said they wanted to buy the stadium was what made me want to get the deal done. It was the best thing for Coventry City.'

And he did get it over the line – but not before many a tear was shed by scores of Coventry City supporters.

One of Sisu's conditions for going ahead with the purchase was that all of the 55,000 shares in the club must be handed over to the new owners.

Families who had held shares in their beloved football club for years – in some cases passed down from fathers and mothers to sons and daughters – would now be forced to part with them. Few would have held on to them in the hope that some day they might be able to sell them on for a profit, but while the monetary value was inconsequential the sentimental value was immeasurable.

An appeal was launched for Sky Blues fans to hand over their shares or risk the extinction of the club. Joe Elliott was tasked with clawing back the shares on behalf of the new owners. Even Mr Coventry City himself, Jimmy Hill, gave up his one share as a public demonstration that all the great and the good connected to Coventry City believed that this move was in the best interests of their football club.

He was followed by club legends Bobby Gould and Gordon Milne, as well as former chairman John Poynton.

The appeal worked and, over the next few months, all the shares came into the possession of Sisu Capital.

But, while the battle to secure the shares was won, the mental scars of leading that appeal clearly remain with Joe Elliott until this day – and will likely stay with him for the rest of his life.

He said: 'When they bought the shares from the directors they had 74 per cent but they made it very clear unless they got the rest then the deal would not happen.

'My treasured shares, along with everybody else's, were handed in for fractions of a penny to make sure it all happened.

'Probably Jimmy Hill giving in his one share showed the fans the way forward and to hand their shares in so the deal could be completed.

'It was tear-jerking. Very often the shares had been in families for generations. It was a very hard decision but it was for the benefit of the football club and the chance for a new beginning.

'Most people handed the shares over reluctantly but with a smile on their face wishing the club well for the future.'

With that, the new owners of Coventry City were firmly installed.

The club had a new chairman in the shape of Ray Ranson and he was making all the right noises.

Sisu had previously failed in their attempts to purchase Southampton and eventually turned their sights to Coventry. But the deal for the Sky Blues clearly wasn't a straightforward process, and Ray Ranson paid tribute to those who made the deal possible when he was interviewed in the immediate aftermath.

Speaking to the *Coventry Telegraph* soon after his appointment as chairman, he said: 'I am delighted. It has been nerve-racking at times. Many times it nearly fell over but thankfully all parties were very positive.

'Special thanks go to Geoffrey Robinson and Joe Elliott for having the stamina to see it through. Without their support, it would never have been done.

'But we got there in the end and hopefully it will be all worthwhile, because we are in it for the long term.'

Asked why Sisu had chosen Coventry City, Ray Ranson explained that the club had a number of the key ingredients the investors were looking for – not least that Coventry was a 'one-club city' and that it had a 'finished stadium'.

Crucially, a pledge to invest £20m in the club was made – but the new chairman was crystal clear about his priorities now he had his feet under the table. Focus would be on the playing side, with promotion the ultimate aim.

Any thoughts of stadium ownership would sit quietly on the back burner under Ray Ranson, who even suggested stadium ownership was not necessarily part of Sisu's long-term plan.

He told the *Coventry Telegraph*: 'It ticked all the boxes for us – a one-team town with a finished stadium, a loyal fan base and we think there is a real chance of developing things here.

'We have a very good relationship with ACL.

'Daniel Gidney and John McGuigan have been very supportive and we thank them for that.'

'There is an option to acquire a 50 per cent share holding by way of acquiring the football club and we fully intend to take up that option and move forward and develop the relationship.

'I don't know when that will happen but let's get the priorities sorted out, trying to get the team up the league and, dare I say it, promotion, and we will worry about that later.

'I wouldn't say the long-term plan is to own the whole of the stadium but, certainly, we see ACL as a valuable asset to both Coventry City Football Club and the people of Coventry, and we will be part of the development of that.'

At the time, the stance of not seeking ownership of the stadium in the long term raised few eyebrows. The Sky Blues had a new owner promising to invest £20m into the playing side of the club and return them to the top flight. It was a huge turnaround from the noises coming out of club just weeks before, when the very existence of the Sky Blues was called into question. So who can blame anyone for taking their eyes off the 'stadium issue' back then?

For the first time in almost a decade, Coventry City fans could look to the future not just with hope, but with expectation.

Ray Ranson added: 'I want to see us promoted as soon as possible. This is a Premiership club – that is why I am here. I'm in it for the long haul.

'There is a hell of a lot of work to be done here and Sisu want to make a success of it.

'I am in the football industry and have been all my life, and a natural progression of that is to try my arm at ownership and trying to assist Sisu in developing a successful football club.

'There has been a lot of talk about them being a hedge fund.

'Yes, they have a hedge fund but they have various funds and this is coming out of the private equity fund and, by its very nature, they are long-term investors.'

But it seems perhaps Sisu didn't realise at the time just how long-term their investment would turn out to be.

Chapter Four

Held to Ranson

C OVENTRY City fans thought they had got one of the best Christmas presents of all time in December 2007, following the takeover by Sisu and the installation of a new chairman who apparently had £20m burning a hole in his pocket.

Ray Ranson wasted no time stamping his authority on the club and made his first major decision when he sacked popular manager Iain Dowie after a 1-0 defeat to fellow Championship strugglers Preston North End.

The former Charlton Athletic boss had suffered a run of five defeats in his previous six league matches prior to getting the chop, but it wasn't the form book which led to the end of Dowie's spell as manager. It was no secret that the two did not see eye to eye over the direction the club should be taking. Ranson was big on youth and developing players, while Dowie tended to favour more experienced heads.

Despite the differences of opinion, and the form book, the timing of the sacking was odd. The Sky Blues were just days away from their biggest game in recent seasons – a fifth-round FA Cup clash with West Midlands rivals West Bromwich Albion. Many fans saw the tie at the Ricoh Arena as extremely winnable, not least because it was against fellow Championship opposition who City had demolished 4-2 at the Hawthorns just two months previously.

But many pointed to the disruption Ranson had caused by dismissing Dowie as one of the major reasons why the Sky Blues eventually crashed to a 5-0 defeat in front of 28,163 supporters.

It was a bumpy start for the new chairman.

He had to act fast to restore the faith of the Sky Blue Army and swiftly appointed former Fulham boss Chris Coleman.

Off the field he worked to assemble his board, which included appointing Coventry kid and former Northern Rock chief executive Gary Hoffman as vice-chairman.

Joe Elliott was rewarded for his efforts with a seat at the boardroom table, while Sisu man Onye Igwe was there as the owners' eyes and ears. Finance chief Mal Brannigan also kept his position – although he was forced to move on just over a year later when a restructuring of the club by the owners ended with him being made redundant.

Gary Hoffman offered his insight into the situation at the club under the new ownership in those early days, weeks, months and years.

He said: 'Before I joined the board, I had received a number of invitations to join it from previous regimes. I had turned them down because the plans and funding were unclear, despite the fact that, for someone born down the road from Highfield Road, it would have been a bit of a boyhood dream to do so.

'[It was] more of an honour in some ways than being invited on to various substantial PLC boards, and alongside the appointments I classify as giving something back, given how lucky I have been and the privileged position I have found myself in.

'Why did I join the board? Of course because I love the club but mainly because I believed the intent and plans set out in Sisu's offer document for the club, including funding approach, which was about building a platform, investing in young talent and creating a sustainable model.

'I met Ray Ranson, who articulated this vision extremely well. I met Onye Igwe, who seemed to have the right intent too.

'I did not do that much due diligence on Sisu but that which I did checked out despite there not being much public information available.

'Several things soon became clear. Sisu's due diligence had been time consuming but poorly undertaken. For example, the significant tax liability had not been properly described and the commercial due diligence on the arrangements with ACL naive.'

He added: 'Given the financial situation at the club, the best situation would actually have been to go into administration at the time Sisu bought it.

'What actually happened was they paid money they shouldn't have paid for the club, their due diligence was terrible and they ended up putting more money in than they thought they would have to.'

But, on the pitch, the first few seasons under Ray Ranson saw Sky Blues supporters treated to some exciting young talent. It was clear Ray Ranson's aim was to develop promising youngsters and move up the league table as the players improved while playing together.

The first indication of the plan came in early 2008 with the arrivals of Walsall defenders Scott Dann and Danny Fox.

More exciting signings followed at the end of the 2007/08 season as the chairman prepared for his first full season in charge by rubber-stamping moves for classy French midfielder Guillaume Beuzelin, highly rated Icelandic youngster Aron Gunnarsson and one of the best young goalkeepers outside the Premier League, Keiren Westwood.

There was also firepower in the shape of former Crystal Palace hotshot Clinton Morrison and Wolves striker Freddy Eastwood, who many hoped could recapture the form which had made him one of the most exciting prospects in the Football League during his prolific spell at Southend United.

Experience was also drafted in, with ex-Liverpool defender Stephen Wright brought to the club on a free transfer after being released by Sunderland.

From 2008 to 2013, I worked for a PR company which helped to produce the matchday programme for the club and also handled various elements of their public relations.

I can honestly say, in all my years working on PR for the club, there was never an easier time to do the job than during the early Sisu years. There was positivity in the air, the likes of which had been sorely absent in the life of Sky Blues supporters. It was a period to savour.

Reminiscing about the early days of Ray Ranson's reign, Joe Elliott said: 'To Sisu's credit, they bought the football club and Ray and Sisu brought in some exciting and good young players: Keiren Westwood, Scott Dann, Danny Fox, Aron Gunnarsson. It was going well.

'They were some great years. We may have got some things wrong, but we got a lot of things right – Ray, Gary and I.'

Gary Hoffman said: 'Early on the strategy, by judgement and luck, went well.

'Buying young talent and developing it, part cashing in, developing more talent. Create a sustainable platform.

'The purchases and development of Dann, Fox, Westwood and Gunnarsson exemplified it.

'We had a debate about the academy. Whether to continue to fund one at a cost of roughly £500,000 a year or use those funds to buy similar players from lower leagues. A fair question.

'Joe Elliot and I persuaded the board to keep the academy. That has borne fruit. Onye initially wanted to close it.'

Elsewhere behind the scenes, there seemed to be a positive relationship developing between CCFC and ACL as well as its joint stakeholders in Coventry City Council and the Higgs Charity. That relationship obviously had its challenges from time to time, but the consensus seemed to be that Ray Ranson was a driving force for much of the positivity being generated in the early days following Sisu's takeover of CCFC.

Then council development boss John McGuigan said: 'Ahead of the takeover, my key advice to Onye was if you are really serious about this, you need to get someone who knows something about football. A few weeks later, I was introduced to Ray Ranson. Ray quickly brought real credibility and confidence.

'He quickly established himself in his chairman's office deep within and part of the ACL open office space. I don't think the public – and particularly CCFC supporters – understood the positive relationships and working together that went on between ACL and predominantly Ray.

'Fairly quickly, ACL and CCFC brought together their back-of-house and common services, such as marketing, ticketing, financial management, grounds maintenance etc.

'In due course, we carried out the financial management of the two independent companies under a joint finance director, someone who had been a long-standing CCFC employee.

'On a personal level, Ray also gained the confidence and trust of the ACL board and ACL's senior managers. Ray was no fool and his blunt and straightforward way of doing things allowed the same approach to be taken by us.

'Ray was a difficult guy to deal with sometimes, but everything was going swimmingly.'

But there were still some significant off-the-pitch problems.

It was clear ACL, the Higgs Charity and the council expected the club's new owners to complete a deal for a half share in the Ricoh Arena relatively quickly after taking over the club.

However, Ray Ranson had made clear his focus was on achieving promotion and that the stadium issue would take a back seat until that objective had been achieved.

John McGuigan and others involved at this time told me they found the approach odd, particularly bearing in mind the signals of intent the authority, ACL and the charity had received from the owners ahead of the deal to secure the football club.

He said: 'I expected them to be 50 per cent shareholders in the Ricoh Arena straight away, but that didn't happen. They always said they wanted to apply the money to building the team.

'The ACL board also invited CCFC to attend our meetings as an observer at that stage, both in anticipation that Sisu would soon buy back the Higgs' ACL shares and that we could further explore how we could better work together.

'But, for whatever reason, Sisu declined to take up this offer. But they did come to the ACL board meetings for specific issues as they arose.'

He added: 'I could never understand why a hedge fund/ venture capitalist didn't make securing an asset as its first priority.

'I constantly asked Onye when they were going to buy back the Higgs' ACL shares. We had expected this to happen straight after they'd completed the purchase of CCFC.

'Onye's only response was 'we need to put money into CCFC first.'

'Sisu had many opportunities to purchase back the original CCFC shares in ACL, especially at the time when their standing was high, but they never did this.

'Unfortunately, the rest is now history, but history that is still alive.'

The situation over the stadium caused some alarm to one member of the club's board, even if the chairman and Sisu's man, Onye Igwe, did not seemed that concerned by the issue. Gary Hoffman echoed John McGuigan's confusion over the failure to secure a stadium deal, which he indicated had already been all but agreed in principle prior to Sisu's takeover.

He said: 'The intent to buy 50 per cent of the stadium operating company early was more of an empty promise.

'The stadium and the football club ownership and management needed reuniting and there was plenty of opportunity to do so on advantageous commercial terms.

'I will never understand why the opportunity was not taken.'

He added: 'They had many opportunities to buy the stadium. There was a formula and they also had the opportunity to match any other bidder within a certain period.

'At various stages, they would have been able to buy the stadium for, I would say, £10m or less.

'It was talked about all the time. But they were always wanting to get it cheaper and cheaper. They hadn't got the money to do it.'

But ACL director Peter Knatchbull-Hugessen had a slightly different take on the situation.

He said: 'That's Gary making an analysis, not the result of any direct discussions. Yes, they had opportunities to buy the stadium.

'But Ray's focus was on the Premiership. He always said 'once we're there we'll come and buy you' and we said 'that's fine."

He added: 'At various points, Onye would say things like 'we want to buy your shares.' At one point he said 'we'll give you half a million'. He was told to go away.

'He did strange things, like on one occasion he sent us a huge bouquet of flowers. I'm not sure what the purpose of it was meant to be.

'I don't think it was that Ray and Onye weren't on the same page, I just don't think Onye knew what he was doing.'

At the end of the 2008/09 season, tension began to emerge between Ray Ranson and Sisu over the way the club was run.

The chairman felt his vision for the club had been undermined by the owners when Sisu pushed for the sales of Scott Dann to Birmingham City for £3.5m and Danny Fox to Celtic for £1.5m.

Such was the chairman's fury at the situation he had to be talked out of resigning by close friend Gary Hoffman and fellow board member Joe Elliott.

There were also issues with players moving in the opposite direction. In 2011, Ray Ranson revealed to the *Coventry Telegraph* that player purchases he viewed as crucial had been blocked by the owners over a perceived lack of willingness to invest further.

The chairman insisted he had the opportunity to secure Newcastle striker Andy Carroll, Sunderland midfielder Jordan Henderson and Chelsea midfielder Jack Cork for a total of under £2m.

He said Sisu blocked any attempt to sign the players permanently, although Cork and Henderson did join the club on loan.

Carroll and Henderson both went on to become fully capped England internationals, with Carroll eventually moving to Liverpool for £35m in 2011 and Henderson following him to Anfield just months later for a fee thought to be between £16m and £20m.

Cork went on to star for the England under-21s and the Great Britain Olympic football team in 2012 before later establishing himself in the Premier League with Southampton.

Speaking to the *Coventry Telegraph* in 2011, Ray Ranson said: 'If they had given me £30m three years ago, we would have been in the Premiership by now or, at the very least, the top of the Championship, and if not I would have held my hands up.

'If I had been given the tools, I could have got Andy Carroll, Jordan Henderson and Jack Cork for less than £2m.

'Andy Thorn [then Coventry's head scout] had been to watch Carroll when he was on loan at Preston before he had got anywhere near Newcastle's first team and he thought he was a raw talent who would develop.

'I made an inquiry to buy him and was told they were looking for £700,000 to £800,000 with a sell-on clause.

'We took Jordan on loan when he was on something like £800 a week and we had an option to buy him and I wanted to buy him, as I did Jack Cork, who we also had an option to buy from Chelsea but, again, they wouldn't do it.

'We could have got the three of them for about £2m and we could have had a team with Westwood in goal, England under-21 international Martin Cranie at right-back, Scott Dann, Ben Turner, Danny Fox, Jordan Henderson, Aron Gunnarsson, Sammy Clingan, Jack Cork, Gary McSheffrey and Andy Carroll up front, and you are not telling me we would be still be in this division with that team.

'The fact is, if they had invested heavily early on when we took over, we could have built a really strong side and acquired our 50 per cent in the Ricoh.

'But instead, they have drip-fed it.'

Despite his obvious reservations, Ray Ranson and the board continued to steer the Sky Blues through the 2009/10 season. But it was far from a success. The Sky Blues finished in 19th position in the Championship under Chris Coleman, the club's lowest league finish in more than 45 years. The team ended the campaign with an embarrassing 4-0 defeat at home to Watford.

At the time, reasons for the team's slump after a promising first season under Coleman were unclear. But subsequent newspaper reports over the bitter divorce process he went through with his now ex-wife might shed some light on why the Welshman might not have been able to focus as much of his energy into the job as he might like.

Coleman was sacked by the chairman days after the end of the season and the hunt for a new manager was on.

Names in the frame included Steve Cotterill, who that season had led Notts County to the League Two title in impressive style, and former player and manager Gary McAllister. Steve Coppell was also touted as a possible successor, along with Gareth Southgate, Alan Curbishley and Tony Mowbray.

But it was former Watford chief Aidy Boothroyd who eventually got the job, with his no-nonsense attitude seemingly a major pull. But not all of the board were convinced.

Gary Hoffman said: 'We made, what turned out to be, not the best managerial choices.

'I was involved in the interview process of one of those – Aidy Boothroyd.

'He was not Ray's first choice but was definitely Onye's, I suspect solely because he was cheaper.'

Despite the reservations from some about Boothroyd's direct style of play, there can be little doubt he made a storming start to the season.

The club put together a fantastic run of form which saw them sitting in fourth position as they played at home in front of 28,184 supporters against Leeds United on 6 November 2010. They lost that game 3-2, but at long last it looked as though Coventry City could finally enjoy a serious promotion challenge.

But the owners were seemingly dissatisfied. The losses being endured by the club were clearly not sustainable and the mood music off the pitch began to change.

Gary Hoffman said: 'It was clear that the funding and talent strategy outlined in Sisu's offer document was no longer the intent.

'Rather, that a very short-term view was being taken to fund players wages from expensive third-party financing. This is where I started to have real differences with Onye.'

It was at this point a number of new faces arrived on the board, much to the surprise of the vice-chairman.

They included former Southampton chairman Ken Dulieu and social media Canadian entrepreneur Leonard Brody.

Sisu seemingly thought the pair could bring fresh ideas to the table as they aimed to stop the club bleeding money at the rate it was.

Gary Hoffman said: 'We were fourth in the Championship, playing Leeds United in front of 29,000.

'The hotel was full, the casino was turning people away. That day, and various away matches where our support was magnificent, demonstrated the commercial potential.

'We had got to that point because Ray Ranson, Joe Elliott and I had stayed with it and worked in the club's interests. It would have fallen apart earlier if we had not.'

He added: 'When Ken Dulieu and Leonard Brody joined the board, I said 'you should not let these people join the board. I have done my research into their backgrounds. One might be good as an internet guru but he is not going to help the business.'

'That was the famous board meeting where there were various things said. They said they thought the club could be breaking even within six months. I said I don't believe it unless you do these things.

'Leonard Brody said he had ten ideas, so I said 'what is your best idea?'

'That was when he talked about 'text a substitute' [an idea which would see supporters text in the substitutions they would want to see made and their choices would be acted on by the manager]. I said even if that were allowed under Football League rules, how do you think that's going to transform the revenues of Coventry City?

'They asked if there was any other business at the meeting and Onye said 'yes, I want to raise the subject of our mascot.'

'The club was going bust and he said 'I think Sky Blue Sam is too fat and it's not setting a good example for children.' That's when Ray said 'Onye, it's a f****** elephant'.

'They were just fiddling around the edges. Another idea was making a Sky Blue Rolls Royce available for wedding hire.

'We spent too much time on things that would not move the dial or were irrelevant.'

In December 2010 there was another dramatic change at the club. Joe Elliott, or 'Mr Coventry' as he is affectionately known in some circles, would be stepping down from the board to take up the role of life president.

He was replaced on the board by former club director, and Coventry public relations guru, John Clarke.

At the time, few batted an eyelid at the decision as the public statements around the move were handled with the sort of slick precision sorely lacking at the club in these more recent times.

As far as the general public were concerned, it seemed to make sense. Joe Elliott had been a long and loyal servant to the club and it was understandable that he might now like to take on a less involved role.

But, privately, it is apparent the decision was not one Joe Elliott had pro-actively taken and came after several months of pressure to step down.

Joe Elliott said: 'The Sisu ownership, through Onye Igwe, were asking me to go in early 2010 to which I said 'I'm not going.'

'On 23 December 2010, they came to me again and said 'we really want you off the board.' It was a strange decision I didn't understand at the time and it was never explained.

'It was even stranger because my skills were bringing in money. I had an excellent relationship with many business people in Coventry and Warwickshire.

'Six weeks before I was formally kicked off the board, I had brought in a sponsorship deal with Lloyds Pharmacy for £300,000.

'After I left the board, I was made life president and I was still allowed to go into the boardroom and sit in the directors' box.

'But that didn't sit easily with me. I would rather be involved in the business aspects rather than just sitting there doing nothing.'

He added: 'I have always tried to do my best for the club and I used my retailing skills to bring in sponsorship and investment.

'I was very honoured to be able to help the club over the years, especially with the academy.'

The move to replace Joe Elliott was obviously not unanimously popular.

Gary Hoffman said: 'I would say that replacing Joe Elliott with John Clarke as the 'local representative' was akin to replacing a Premier League player with one from Division One in terms of experience set, football knowledge and local contacts and influence.

'I remember John promising to the board that he would bring in £500,000 of funding within six months. I left the board immediately after the promise, but my guess is none of that was delivered.'

Less than two months later, the vice-chairman decided to blow the final whistle on his relationship with Sisu and his time on the club's board. He had become disillusioned with the change of direction in the owner's strategy for running the club and clearly found it difficult to see eye to eye with both new and existing board members.

The tipping point was believed to be when the club agreed to loan the highly rated midfielder, academy graduate, Conor Thomas, to Liverpool with a view to a £1m move – although that never materialised and Thomas's career subsequently stalled after a long-running battle with injuries.

Hoffman also had reservations about the financing methods being employed by Sisu and a lack of certainty over whether the wages of coaches and staff would be paid on a month-to-month basis.

In February 2011, he formally resigned from the club's board.

He said: 'They wanted me to leave in the end [and] it was somewhat mutual.

'I said to them there were decisions being made on players I didn't agree with. But the bottom line is that I felt I was being misled, along with other board members.

'They would say one thing they were going to do in a board meeting and then do something different.

'I said I cannot serve on a board where the owners are not being honest with the directors on the board.

'One example was I asked if we were recruiting a chief executive and was told no. Then one of Sisu's employees tells me they've issued a contract to someone.'

He added: 'I differed on business strategy, playing approach, funding plans and areas of focus/priority.

'Onye believed that we needed to work to create a global Sky Blue brand for sports and not just football. Whilst I applaud visionaries, I thought we should concentrate on Cheylesmore, Radford, Bedworth etc first.

'There are still too many people born and/or living in Coventry supporting other teams. Building relationships with the local community is a key part of this. Just because you have a portfolio of businesses in China, Hong Kong and France doesn't mean there are synergies with them.

'It started off well with the purchase of young players with potential. It was always the intention that some be sold on in order to create funding headroom for player trading.

'But Onye did not understand the relationship between players' wages, potential, contract length and value to the company. Refusal to extend contracts and/or increase wages resulted in players leaving us for significantly less than they should have done, Westwood and Gunnarsson being prime examples.

'Funding strategy was unclear and not connected to the original commitment. I argued for either a clear commitment to fund to push for the Premier League, or funding for stability; or cutting costs radically if no funding was available.

'What we had was none of these. Rather, a 'robbing Peter to pay Paul' method. Onye would not commit to the board that next month's wages would be paid and that we needed third-party funding.

'He said it was to keep us on our toes. To be fair if third-party funding did not arrive, Sisu pulled a rabbit out of the hat at the last minute.

'Too often third-party funding was arranged with exorbitant interest rates and finder fees, like funding a house mortgage on credit card debt.

'On top of this, Onye employed brand and business consultants in pursuit of the 'global and digital dream', spending well over £200,000 on such fruitless efforts.

'Meanwhile, local suppliers were kept waiting for many months for their relatively small amounts of money, which was not good for local relationships.'

As things were being shaken up behind the scenes, the team's play-off charge had fallen off a cliff.

The Sky Blue Army's party had turned into an epic hangover as it crashed to a premature end. Nobody could quite explain why, but there was the suggestion that Boothroyd's direct style of play had been 'found out' by opposition managers.

There were also rumours that Boothroyd had lost the dressing room. A performance of 'the worm' dance move at the club's Christmas party had apparently undermined his authority as a hard taskmaster.

On 14 March 2011, Boothroyd was sacked by chairman Ray Ranson after a run of poor results which saw the club win only once in 16 league games.

Coventry City's new beginning was rapidly falling apart. The owners scrambled around to assemble a new board after Ray Ranson indicated he would stay on to steady the ship.

But the storm had not yet passed. Ranson was clearly unhappy and, in an apparently orchestrated move, he announced his resignation just minutes before a press conference was scheduled to be held to unveil Coventry City's new-look board.

He left in March 2011, complaining that Sisu had failed to give him the tools he needed to do his job.

Reflecting on the news of Ranson's departure, John McGuigan said: 'With Ray leading, things were moving forward in a positive way.

'I was therefore very surprised to receive an urgent phone call from an ACL executive to say 'Ray has just told us he's leaving immediately and would have nothing more to do with Sisu and CCFC.'

'He wouldn't say any more, but clearly there must have been a final blow-up in terms of his relationship with Sisu.

'Obviously there was then major public and private questioning about what happened and who did what to whom, but I never found out exactly what had happened.

'Like many others, I heard lots of speculation and rumour. Only Ray Ranson can really tell us what happened, but I assume he'd signed some confidentiality agreement with Sisu to remain silent.'

Peter Knatchbull-Hugessen said: 'It was fine under Ray and Daniel Gidney [then ACL chief executive]. They worked together and it functioned.

'The club got two-thirds of the way to achieving their objective of promotion and then Sisu bottled it. Joy must have realised Onye had been leading her down an expensive garden path.

'Her taking control and taking it away from Ranson is the thing that killed it.

'If she had taken it away from Onye and left Ranson, they could have achieved it.

'I think, at that point, they were preparing to put the club into administration, but they wanted someone else to push them.'

Chapter Five

'Best board ever'

I T'S March 2011 and Coventry City FC's owners have called a flashy press conference to unveil their 'best board ever'. But the new board hasn't even been announced and a spanner is immediately thrown into the works as outgoing chairman Ray Ranson – who had initially agreed to stay on as an advisor – resigns just 30 minutes before the press conference is due to be held at the Ricoh Arena.

It was obviously a deliberately orchestrated move by a clearly unhappy man, designed to cause the new owners problems.

The club was manager-less, without a chairman and seemingly without direction.

But Coventry City fans were reassured that everything would be OK and that better times lay beyond the horizon – despite the fact the club was perilously close to the relegation zone and teetering on the brink of administration.

In came Paul Clouting, a former Ipswich Town CEO, as the club's new chief executive, and John Clarke, a board member in the 1990s and the local voice, as vice-chairman. Canadian internet expert Leonard Brody filled another position along with Ken Dulieu, who was made chairman, having previously been chairman at Southampton. Sisu man Onye Igwe also kept his position on the board.

This had already been a turbulent period for the club. In recent months, the club had got through three finance directors in Mal Brannigan, Ed Baker and John Street; two commercial directors in Nathan Kosky and Brian Phillpotts, a former commercial director at the Premier League; and a commercial manager in Jas Sodhi.

The club had also shed four other directors, including Sisu-appointed Mike Parton, who is understood to have resigned over a lack of clarity on the business plan; Walter Bosco, who was briefly put on the board by Sisu then taken off; and former vice-chairman Gary Hoffman, who publicly resigned after losing confidence in Sisu. Joe Elliott had also been forced off the board and made life president.

In addition, board secretary John Tomlinson had resigned while Onye Igwe's personal assistant, Helen Chandler, had also quit.

In a barbed comment aimed at the owners' handling of the club during this period, Gary Hoffman said: 'I might be wrong, Ray might be wrong, the council might be wrong, a succession of CEOs, CFOs and commercial directors might be wrong. But it is unlikely we are all wrong.'

Former chairman Geoffrey Robinson was also clearly far from impressed at a perceived lack of progress since Sisu's takeover.

Speaking to the *Telegraph* at the time of the board changes, he said: 'It shows that people have got no confidence in them and there's no future.

'The people either go or they sack them because they have got no plan for the business.

'It's death by a thousand cuts – death by inactivity, by not spending any money and not doing anything.

'All they have done so far is fund losses which they are responsible for creating.

'We never had losses of this scale.'

He added: 'The football club is a total disaster.

'They have made a total mess of it – a disgraceful mess – and they should find a good home for the club as soon as possible, write off their losses, which they are entirely responsible for themselves, and let's get the club back on the up.

'With this ownership and these people, the club has no future.

'I have grave concerns about the club because the owners have turned out to be an absolute waste of time and space.

'The club and the city deserve better than they have produced.

'They gave all sorts of statements about what they intended to do for the club and how they were going to get us back to the Premier League, all the usual stuff, and I believed it.

'Of course you can't, in those circumstances, get a written undertaking because you can't do anything if it doesn't come off.

'But I am bitterly disappointed, as disappointed as any man possibly could be.'

The new board, brought in to steady the ship and instil confidence, seemed not to have the desired effect after making some bizarre public statements within the first few days of taking over.

Paul Clouting described the club as a 'basket case' in an interview with the *Coventry Telegraph*.

He said: 'It doesn't take a rocket scientist looking from the outside to look at this business and argue that it is a bit of a basket case in the sense of it is losing money and it is not as successful as arguably a club of this stature should be.'

He added: 'The company is haemorrhaging money so the first job was, how do we stop the club going into administration?'

There were also criticisms that the new-look board was too far removed from the club because many of them lived in other cities or countries. And Clouting did little to reassure fans that the board would offer a hands-on approach.

He said: 'Will Leonard be at every single game? No he won't because he has got other things to do and a life in the States.

'Will Ken be at every game? No, because he is in Portugal.

'Will I be at every game? Probably not. I live in Ipswich. But I am not interested in second best and I am very competitive with myself about what I do and what I don't do, and how successful I can be, and hopefully the value I can bring to the business.'

Having demonstrated such clear commitment in his first interview as the club's chief executive, it's perhaps not surprising that he left the club after just seven months at the top, opting for a quieter life running a golf and country club.

Despite his infamous 'text a sub' suggestion in his inaugural board meeting, Leonard Brody did seem to be a popular appointment with fans in the beginning. This was not least down to his willingness to interact with fans online – although he later mysteriously disappeared from social media network Twitter when things continued on a downward trajectory.

Following his appointment to the board, he offered a scathing view about what had gone wrong under Sisu's time in charge of the club.

He told the *Coventry Telegraph*: 'In three years and £30m, where did it get you? Virtually in the same place. Somebody has to be accountable.

'The fingers can't be pointed at the investors. The fingers have to be pointed at the people responsible for running it. You don't see CEOs of companies turning round and blaming their investors for lack of performance.

'That doesn't come from the investor, it comes from the team that was responsible for stewarding this club for the community. And the results weren't there.

'We mustn't sugar-coat this. People should know the truth.

'What you were witnessing was three years of a dispute between shareholders, people who had different visions and different ideas about where the club was and what they wanted to do.

'The key difference here is unity. You now have the shareholders dispute resolved and a new board that is committed not only to the team but also to the community.'

But that commitment, it seems, only stretched so far, as Leonard Brody departed just eight months after joining the board citing 'time constraints'.

One thing that did appear to be clear under the new leadership was that the focus had shifted to acquiring a stake in the Ricoh Arena as well as driving down the club's debts.

It's perhaps understandable that a club in such financial difficulty would desperately be searching for assets to act as security. Asked why there had been a sudden change of focus in relation to the stadium, Onye Igwe said at the time: 'It's a question of having a management team who could deliver on that and so far that has not happened.

'Maybe you could say we didn't move hard enough and fast enough to do that, but the new board recognises it as a day-one priority.'

He added: 'We have already invested several millions of pounds and we haven't taken anything out.

'When we came in, we had the view of improving the way the business operates. It is clear that has not been successful but we've got a lot of very good ideas that, up until now, with all that's been going on, have been lost.

'I am convinced we've got the right board in place. We thought long and hard about the qualities and skills we needed and they've got a lot of experience and some great ideas on how we can move forward.'

While Onye Igwe might have been convinced of his own skills and his ability to take the club forward, it seems others above him were not. Just over a year later, Igwe's departure from the club was confirmed – although it appeared he had not been actively involved for some time. He was also no longer listed as a director of Sisu Capital by April 2012.

But Onye Igwe lasted longer than the club's new head of football operations – or chairman. Ken Dulieu enjoyed a brief but colourful spell as top dog after proclaiming himself as the man to rescue the club. In various press interviews, he claimed he had talked the owners out of putting the club into administration and that they were hours, if not days, away from pulling the plug.

He went on to earn the nickname 'Orange Ken' from supporters on account of his perma-tan look.

Highlights of his reign included arranging a pre-season training camp to Vale do Lobo in Portugal, where they trained on a pitch at the rear of the grounds to his luxury villa.

He was also pictured wearing training kit with his initials on and taking a seat on the bench during a match.

That incident ultimately led to his downfall and he resigned in December 2011 citing it as a 'gross error of judgement'.

Just over 12 months previously, the Sky Blues faced Leeds United in front of a bumper Ricoh Arena crowd aiming to cement their place in the Championship play-offs.

But, bizarrely, he left insisting that he had turned the club around and left it in a better place despite it being in turmoil off the pitch and struggling to avoid relegation on the field.

In a strange interview with the *Coventry Telegraph* at the time of his departure, he said he believed the Ricoh Arena situation had progressed thanks to his background in the Northern Ireland conflict and that he was never in it for the long term

He said: 'I used to look after security operations in Northern Ireland and it was a nightmare.

'But, ultimately, people did start talking and resolving their differences and it is actually quite a nice place to go now.'

He added: 'I was never going to be here long-term. My job was interim to turn the business around and we are in front of budget and turned the business around substantially, and now the building blocks are in place and we can move forward with a lot more confidence than we had in March.'

The raft of departures over the months eventually left John Clarke as the sole surviving director of the football club's 'best board ever'. He continued in his role as vice-chairman until March 2013 – just days before the club did finally enter administration.

On the pitch, the 'best board ever' had appointed chief scout Andy Thorn as permanent manager after he achieved some promising results as caretaker, although the decision was also widely viewed as financially motivated at the time – perhaps unsurprising against the backdrop of the club's financial struggles.

He led them to safety in his first few months in charge, one of the few positives supporters could take from the period.

There were appointments off the pitch too during 2011 – including some faces which became extremely familiar to Sky Blues fans over the next few months and years.

First through the revolving door were investment bankers Tim Fisher and Mark Labovitch – the latter of whom had previously headed up former prime minister Tony Blair's 'Firerush Ventures' as chief operating officer.

They were joined shortly afterwards by Steve Waggott, who had been persuaded to join the club by Tim Fisher after the two had worked together previously at Charlton Athletic.

Tim Fisher later revealed in an interview with the *Coventry Telegraph* the reasons behind his appointment – indicating Sisu boss Joy Seppala had decided to take a more 'hands-on' approach and that his role involved delivering promotion and securing a stake in the Ricoh Arena.

He said: 'Joy Seppala is now hands-on. I speak to her every single day and, by the way, she comes to games and, by the way, she stood in front of the players and told them and has been very clear in what it is she expects, what the fans expect.

'We presented a three-year plan to Sisu, including the funding requirements. That plan was signed off by Sisu. I have been asked to deliver the plan, certainly the first part of the plan, which I am relishing.

'We are going to look to get promoted, become a community club and a club which has the academy at its cornerstone and leverages the talent that comes through.

'If we don't perform, do well, get promoted, complete the transaction, I don't get paid.'

The raft of changes and strategy was a sign that the owners had not been happy with the way things had been run. Publicity-shy Sisu boss Joy Seppala has not given many public statements on the way things have unfolded at the the club, but in 2012 she did speak to the *Coventry Telegraph* and, in 2016, she met with fans to discuss issues of the past. She indicated that she had 'put a lot of faith in the wrong people', describing it as a 'tragedy'.

During the 2012 interview, she was asked to reflect on the deal to take over the football club and said: 'People did the due diligence and for all intents and purposes we took calculated risks.

'What I can say definitively is that since I've become involved in the last two years, I have not regretted any of the decisions that we've made.

She added: 'In a multitude of ways, this has been one of the most extraordinary professional experiences I've had. I've learned from it, and I don't regret anything.

'If I was asked, 'Would I make the same investment again that we made in 2007, I would say, 'No.''

There would be plenty of activity to keep supporters interested elsewhere off the pitch during the next few months – not least thanks to former vice-chairman Gary Hoffman and life president Joe Elliott.

Hoffman had set about securing potential investors with the aim of launching a takeover bid for the club. He was being supported in his endeavours by the club's life president, which did not sit well with those still on the board of Coventry City. Chairman Ken Dulieu ordered Joe Elliott to step down and, when he refused, the board took the decision to suspend the Sky Blues stalwart.

Speaking shortly after the club had decided to freeze him out, Joe Elliott said: 'I am disappointed to have been asked to step aside but have agreed to do so in the hope that it helps our beloved Sky Blues find investment for the future.

'I have not been stripped but it is a sort of suspension of duties.

'I have always served the club with passion and love and share the hopes and dreams with all our fans, and I will continue in my many roles within the club.

'As far as I am concerned, to step aside means on a temporary basis.

'If I have stepped aside, I would hope to resume in that role. I would hope it is on a makeshift basis.

'It's down to them and I have agreed to conform with that while discussions are taking place.

'I am not overly happy about it but I am prepared to do it to help the whole thing.'

In August 2011, Gary Hoffman lodged his first formal CCFC takeover bid. Secret meetings were held with a view to a £30m takeover which would have included securing half of stadium company ACL and strengthening the squad.

But the deal would have seen Sisu given just £1 to cut their losses and walk away.

At the time, the identities of those behind the consortium was kept secret. But details were eventually leaked and it emerged that Ken Bruce, a retired lawyer and a former chairman of the investment vehicle Investing in Sport, had been present at the meetings.

The football men behind the bid were former Coventry City player Sam Allardyce and Howard Wilkinson, who had twice been the England national team's caretaker manager.

City fans looking on from the outside eventually saw what came to happen over the next few days as a farce, as the offer was seemingly mocked by club officials for not being presented 'on headed notepaper'.

Gary Hoffman said: 'We met confidentially with Ken Dulieu and Paul Clouting.

'Ken Dulieu also met separately with me and said 'I think I could get a deal through Joy as long as I stay on as chairman.'

'At the end of a constructive discussion, we agreed that nothing would be said publicly and shook hands on that and on trying to find a way forward.

'Within an hour, the names of some of the individuals had been leaked to the press and a formal statement from the club was put out saying nothing had been put forward.

'I had also agreed with Ken Dulieu that anything in writing should be in the form of an outline proposal for him to discuss with the board and not naming the parties, although he was aware of who was involved. He then publicly criticised us for producing a proposal in this form 'not on headed notepaper'.

'Soon after the meeting, Ken Bruce received a lawyers' letter accusing individuals of breaking Football League rules and asking about my relationship with any potential deal in terms of position and financial interest.

'This goes to the core of the misunderstanding of motives – I have already said I would never take a penny from CCFC. Indeed, I left my associate director a £50,000 'gift' in the club despite having the associated privileges confiscated.

'Unsurprisingly, eventually, Ken Bruce and associates gave up given how they were treated.

'Other potential investors that we nurtured, and which Coventry fans would have been excited by the identity of, were given similar treatment and short shrift.'

Speaking shortly after the meeting, Ken Dulieu indicated talks had fallen apart. He also raised questions over whether those already involved with other clubs could realistically complete a takeover – suggesting it would be against Football League rules.

He said: 'There have been several meetings with Gary Hoffman on this matter. He and Joe Elliott attended along with four other people.

'We had been led to believe by an e-mail from Gary on 8 August that this would be a meeting with his principal investors. We were therefore surprised and disappointed to learn that no principal investors were present and there is still no transparency as to their identity.

'There was a frank exchange of views. No formal offer was put on the table, which is what we had been asking for. Gary's previous indicative offer of £1 for the club is totally unacceptable. I can fully understand people being frustrated at the outcome of this meeting as it is becoming a long and drawn-out saga.

'It cannot go on forever because it is not fair on our supporters, who have been led to believe that something concrete will happen.

'We have a business to run and want to put 100 per cent of our efforts into supporting Andy Thorn, Steve Harrison [then assistant manager] and the team, and turning the club around. Therefore the position remains the same – Sisu continue to fund the club.'

With the identities of the potential investors leaked and questions raised over the legality of the takeover bid, those involved walked away.

But Hoffman and Elliott were not willing to give up the fight to buy Coventry City. Talks continued with potential investors behind the scenes, and by January 2012 Gary Hoffman had apparently attracted a group of Chinese billionaires who had declared an interest in the Sky Blues.

They were the Wanda Group, which had assets of £20bn and were headed by Wang Jianlin, a 57-year-old entrepreneur whose personal fortune of £4bn made him the sixth richest person in China.

Wanda had a commercial and leisure-based portfolio. They owned 49 shopping malls, 40 department stores, 28 five-star hotels and 80 cinemas in China and had created the world's largest chain of cinemas by buying America's AMC group for £1.64bn.

Acquiring a League One club would not seem to be a tempting prospect for a conglomerate of their size, but they presumably saw it as a chance to give their brand a UK foothold on a prime site in the heart of England with space to develop hotel, commercial and leisure facilities. At the time, they employed over 50,000 people.

Wanda, which translated as 'a thousand roads lead here', also already had an interest in football. In 1994 they acquired Dalian FC, changing their name to Dalian Wanda and becoming national champions in the first fully professional season in China.

Wang had pulled out of the game in 2000 after criticising Chinese referees for match fixing, but Wanda continued to sponsor the Chinese Super League with a £50m package.

At the start of 2012, Gary Hoffman had begun official talks with the club over his second takeover offer.

A statement from Tim Fisher, chief executive of Coventry City, confirmed: 'We have had a proposal letter from Gary Hoffman and his associates looking to discuss the future of the football club.

'We have agreed to meet in the near future to talk through both their intentions and plans and to share our own plans for the future of Coventry City.

'We will devote appropriate time and effort to these discussions – but it will not distract us from our ongoing efforts to improve things on and off the field.'

But those talks ultimately fell away by early 2013, with Gary Hoffman suggesting the investors were put off by the legal row which erupted in the following months over the Ricoh Arena.

He said: 'They were put off by all the litigation which was ongoing. Everyone is, aren't they?'

In 2015, the Wanda Group bought a 20 per cent stake in Athletico Madrid. At the time of writing, they were linked with a potential takeover bid for Coventry City's Midlands rivals West Bromwich Albion.

On the pitch, things had taken a turn for the worse – not helped by the fact a transfer embargo had been slapped on the club after they failed to file their accounts on time.

Andy Thorn was unable to repeat the miracles performed at the end of the previous season and the team were relegated to League One on 21 April 2012 after rolling over at home to Doncaster Rovers and suffering a 2-0 defeat.

They bowed out of the league with a hefty 4-0 defeat to Southampton at St Mary's – perhaps the clearest indication of how far the club had fallen at that time. The Saints were seen as a similar club in many ways, and one with which many City fans feel an affinity after many years of battling relegation together in the top flight. Coincidentally, Sisu had unsuccessfully attempted to take over Southampton before taking the reins at Coventry.

Now the two clubs found their futures on wildly different trajectories, with Southampton heading back to the Premier League and the Sky Blues relegated to their lowest level in nearly 50 years.

Analysing the club's downfall at the time Andy Turner, the *Coventry Telegraph's* Coventry City reporter, said: 'There is more talk of liquidation than administration.

'Sisu are estimated to have spent £35m to £40m on the club since they took over in late 2007.

'At that time, the club was losing about £500,000 per month. Those losses have come down through cost-cutting – but that hasn't helped the team. Sisu came in with good intentions. But instead of building a squad, outstanding prospects were sold, including Danny Fox and Scott Dann. New contracts for Keiren Westwood, Aron Gunnarsson and Marlon King were never agreed, meaning they all left for nothing.

'The great killer was last summer – nine players out, three in. You can't survive by doing that. Had Marlon King still been here, Coventry would still be a Championship club. He was offered five grand a week more by Birmingham but the owners were not willing to match the terms.'

Chapter Six

Charity begins at home

BY early 2012, it was clear the owners of Coventry City had changed their strategy. The ultimate aim was to drive down losses and secure an asset which could provide some security to their investment.

Perhaps partly due to focus being taken off the pitch, the team had sank to its lowest level in almost half a century, with the club's relegation to the third tier of English football.

Conspiracy theories circulated at the time that the owners had stuck with Andy Thorn as manager, despite the club plummeting towards relegation from the Championship, because they wanted the club to be relegated. Fans took to online message boards to cite elaborate theories about reduced running costs in the lower leagues.

But not everyone bought into this tin foil hat conspiracy theory. The rewards for being in the Championship – financial and otherwise – clearly far outweigh any perceived benefit from the lower running costs associated with League One football.

But the cost-cutting drive continued and Tim Fisher, an experienced investment banker, was the man tasked with getting the club's finances in order – and leading on the stadium talks.

The stadium issue was not entirely straightforward, of course. In summary, the situation was this.

The freehold of the Ricoh Arena (the land itself) is owned by Coventry City Council.

Arena Coventry Limited (ACL) operated the Ricoh Arena and was the business side of the Ricoh Arena. ACL was jointly owned by Coventry City Council and the Alan Edward Higgs Charity, who both had 50 per cent stakes in the company.

Something that will prove important later on is this: ACL had borrowed approximately £22m from Yorkshire Bank in order to fund the purchase of a lease to operate the arena from the council. This loan, mentioned in Chapter One, started life as a loan from the council before the bank took it on shortly afterwards. But let's move on for now.

The ACL company was originally envisaged as being a joint partnership between the council and Coventry City FC, but financial difficulties forced the club to sell its shares to the Higgs Charity for £6.5m in 2003.

Coventry City retained an option to buy the charity's shares at any point in the future, with the value determined by a formula – believed to be 75 per cent of the 50 per cent at the original price and two per cent annual interest on the remaining 25 per cent.

Coventry City FC also paid ACL about £1.3m in annual rent. The rent was set to comply with European state aid rules and was based on how much financing would have cost if the club had paid for the stadium part of the Arena on its own.

The club had a lease to play at the Ricoh Arena, but it had sacrificed its right to income from non-matchday events and matchday revenue such as parking, food and drink when it sold its share in ACL to the Higgs Charity.

The original model envisaged that the club would be in the Premier League, be a shareholder in ACL and therefore share in profits. Initial forecasts predicted the club's income from ACL would far outweigh rent payments.

But the club had never reached the top flight or become a partner in ACL and the rent was now a huge issue for a club struggling in the lower reaches of the Football League.

In 2012, after almost a decade, Coventry City appeared to be seriously interested in buying back their stake in ACL for the first time. They were desperate to find a solution to their financial problems with the club on the brink of insolvency.

Tim Fisher, who was then chief executive, and Joy Seppala, Sisu chief executive, took the lead on the stadium talks from the club's perspective while a possible rent reduction was also on the table. Negotiations with Higgs Charity bosses to discuss a potential deal began in March 2012 with charity trustee Paul Harris and clerk Peter Knatchbull-Hugessen heavily involved.

But there was an immediate bump in the road as the club stopped paying its legally agreed £1.3m annual rent to the stadium company. The rent money was an important income stream for ACL as they needed to make regular payments to Yorkshire Bank in order to service the £22m loan they had taken out.

This move by the football club has been hotly debated in courtrooms ever since – with Sisu's lawyers insisting it was a 'rent holiday' agreed with ACL, while lawyers for the council have branded it a 'rent strike'.

The fact ACL's shareholders were entertaining talks with the club's owners while the football club was putting the Ricoh Arena firm under financial pressure by not paying the agreed rent clearly did not sit well with everybody involved.

ACL chairman David Allvey quit the board in May as the crunch talks with the Sky Blues continued.

David Allvey was widely understood to be against a deal with the football club's owners, not least because he was unhappy with the way Sisu had approached the rent dispute.

It was also understood that Allvey was extremely upset and concerned about the future of Coventry City FC and the relationship between Sisu and the stadium.

Additionally, it was reported that Allvey believed ACL should force the Sky Blues to pay full rent under the terms of their existing contract.

Coventry City Council leader John Mutton confirmed at the time that there had been disagreements concerning ACL's ongoing failure to make expected profits from commercial activities and warned that ACL profits were likely to be 'very small' that year.

ACL's accounts for the year up to 31 May 2011 showed a profit of just £470,000 – ahead of the withdrawal of the club's £1.3m annual rent.

Coun Mutton also warned that lowering the £100,000-a-month rent to the relegated Sky Blues would plunge ACL into the red – although senior ACL figures disputed this at the time.

A statement released by ACL at the time of David Allvey's resignation said the chairman planned to retire after six years with the company.

It read: 'David has decided it would be best to take the opportunity to leave now because a difference of opinion has emerged between him and the shareholders over future strategy.'

David Allvey said: 'I wish the company every success on the next stage of its development and am sure the Ricoh Arena will continue to thrive as a premier destination venue for the benefit of Coventry and beyond.'

Speaking after news of David Allvey's resignation had broken, Cllr Mutton said: 'I am aware there are one or two differences of opinion over a strategy for how to maximise use of the Ricoh Arena. The difference of opinion is not between the two shareholders, the council and the Higgs charity.

'The Ricoh is only achieving 50 per cent of its potential. Profits again this year are going to be very small.

'ACL hasn't been able to attract developers to build hotels nearby. That's costing us £2m in conference facilities a year.

'The one thing potential conference investors always tell is we've only got 70-odd bedroom spaces and there are no hotels nearby.

'If there is an attempt to lower rent for the football club, it could mean putting ACL into a non-profit making position.

'Someone has got to take ACL forward. It can't stay static. It's not a criticism of anyone, or any of the staff. It's the reality of life.

'I know they are working hard to attract other events to the Ricoh. They keep putting bids in, but things are being turned down, although not everything by any means."

Oddly, this period of chaos behind the scenes coincided with arguably the most impressive period in the Ricoh Arena's history.

In June 2012, ACL handed over the keys to the Ricoh Arena to the London Organising Committee for the Olympic and Paralympic Games.

A total of 12 Olympic football matches would be played at the stadium, briefly renamed the City Of Coventry Stadium – with an unfortunate acronym of COCS – over eight days in the summer.

Daniel Gidney, chief executive of ACL, said: 'This will be a really proud moment in our history and we are honoured to be the only Midlands venue to have been chosen to host an Olympic event in any sport or discipline.'

And it certainly was a proud moment as thousands of supporters travelled from across the globe to see Olympic sport played in Coventry.

It also provided a much-needed to boost to ACL's coffers. The 2012/13 accounts showed turnover doubled for the period thanks largely to the Olympics, although profit margins still struggled, with the firm recording profit of just £775,465, which was actually down from £1.09m in the previous year.

The Olympic Games may have helped the stadium firm in the short term – but, as Mark Labovitch said on more than one occasion, when trying to underline the fragile state of ACL's finances 'you can't have an Olympic Games every year'.

Perhaps sensing the uncertain times ahead, and having just delivered the biggest event in the Ricoh Arena's history, Daniel Gidney left his role as ACL's chief executive shortly after London 2012.

He became the second high-profile figure to quit the firm following the resignation of chairman David Allvey.

During this period, I was still working for a PR firm in Coventry and, as well as undertaking work for CCFC, my then employers also served the Ricoh Arena and Yorkshire Bank – as well as performing *ad hoc* work for the council and the Higgs Charity. It was a difficult position but one which provided enormous insight into what was going on behind the scenes.

Daniel Gidney left in October to take up the position of chief executive at Lancashire County Cricket Club.

There was obvious tension between ACL and club officials during this time – as demonstrated by the resignation of David Allvey. The football club and ACL were also sharing office space, which was far from ideal in such a toxic environment.

Antagonism was rife, with one such example being the removal of free parking for all club employees after rent payments were missed. ACL officials ordered all the parking validation machines to be confiscated from the club's offices, a seemingly petty and unhelpful move for the sake of scoring a few points and saving a relatively small amount of money.

Back on the stadium ownership front, discussions had reached the stage where Sisu and the charity were able to agree indicative terms for the charity's 50 per cent share in ACL. The heads of terms agreement was recorded in a document dated 18 June 2012.

This term sheet outlined a proposed deal which would see Sisu, or another Sisu group company, purchase the charity's

50 per cent interest in ACL for a total cash consideration of £1.5m, payable immediately upon completion of the share purchase.

Following completion, it was envisaged that further payments would follow over a period of ten years. Sisu suggested this would work by giving the charity a stake in ACL to the value of £4m, which would be paid down through annual payments over the ten-year period.

This looked like a great deal for all concerned. The charity would cash in on its share, the club would get a reduced rent (it was hoping for around £200,000 per annum), the council would get increased revenues as AEG, which runs the former Millennium Dome in London, would be brought in to help operate the stadium. There were, of course, a lot of ifs and buts, the main one being the charity getting a fair price for its share.

But the plan was not set in stone.

The term sheet contained a statement that read: 'Sisu would consider an alternative structure to that of preferred equity.

'The parties will work together to achieve a solution in respect of suitable alternatives.'

The indicative 'heads of terms' agreement also granted Sisu a period of 30 days to complete 'due diligence' (financial investigations) and ensure everything was in order and that the Ricoh Arena business was in a satisfactory condition. Four conditions had to be met before the deal could be rubber-stamped.

The first was that Sisu would strike a deal with Yorkshire Bank to pay off ACL's loan.

The second condition depended on favourable advice being given by the charity's advisers about the terms of the deal. The third depended on approval of the deal by the Charity Commission and the fourth condition on approval of the transaction by Coventry City Council, which had the right to veto any deal for the charity's shares.

No specific target date for completion of the deal was agreed, other than all parties would work to get it over the line 'as soon as possible'.

The heads of terms document added: 'This offer [meaning the offer made by Sisu to purchase shares] is non-binding and subject to due diligence.'

But the exclusivity period expired on 31 July 2012 without any share purchase agreement being concluded. Neither was there any agreement to extend the exclusivity period. The deal appeared to be off.

An e-mail from Higgs Charity clerk Peter Knatchbull-Hugessen sent to Laura Deering of Sisu, which became public, responded to a request from the club's owners to extend the exclusivity period. It all but confirmed the charity believed the talks had failed over a perceived lack of security and it stated that the charity wanted to remain open to other approaches for their shares.

It read: 'The Trustees have seen no progress towards a transaction with Sisu. For the transaction to move forward, you will recall, there was work needed to provide better security for any annuity stream that might be agreed.

'The Trustees have seen no evidence that any thought has been given to this fundamental matter. Had they had any proposal to overcome this hurdle, they would now consider an extension of the period of exclusivity.

'The Trustees wish to remain open to other approaches, should they be made, as there is little evidence that the period of exclusivity has been used to any effect.'

But why? What had gone so dreadfully wrong in the space of six weeks that ultimately led to all sides walking away from the deal? The negotiations became the subject of a High Court hearing in Birmingham in April 2014, which provided valuable insight into exactly what went on. I sat through it all for three days, and it was actually refreshing to have some facts presented by a highly qualified judge without the usual ambiguity I had to contend with on a daily basis.

The hearing came about as a result of the Higgs Charity claiming Sisu owed them £29,000 as a result of these failed negotiations – in order to cover their costs. They were ultimately unsuccessful after Mr Justice Leggatt ruled that 'neither party had any appetite to seek to pursue any negotiations based on the term sheet to attempt to conclude such a deal' after August 2012.

Sisu, seemingly somewhat put out by the suggestion that they should cover the charity's costs for the failed negotiations, launched a counter-claim for £290,000.

The judge threw this counter-claim out on the first day of the three-day hearing, branding it 'hopeless'. During the hearing, Sisu's own barrister, Rhodri Thompson admitted there was an element of 'tit-for-tat' in Sisu's counter-claim.

Barrister John Brennan, representing the charity, said the counter-claim was disproportionate.

He said: 'The counter-claim is based on a case which has no prospect of success. This counter-claim is not to pick up a shield, but to wield a sword.'

Judge Leggatt evidently agreed and, during the hearing, questioned the value of Sisu's claim and the timing.

He said: 'Where he has limited his claim to £29,000, it seems the sky is the limit for you. Negotiations seem, for the most part, to have failed... they had effectively come to an end.

'Then, months down the line, when a new transaction comes in, it seems to trigger a costs payment. It doesn't seem obvious why to me.'

But back to the talks and why they broke down. You won't be surprised to learn that both sides didn't see eye to eye on that.

Sisu insisted a later deal, which involved the council taking over the Yorkshire Bank loan to ACL, killed off any hope of a deal with the Higgs Charity.

But the judge dismissed this argument, insisting that talks between the Higgs Charity and Sisu had fallen away months before the council struck a deal with ACL and Yorkshire Bank.

Mr Leggatt said: 'The negotiations ceased by mutual consent or acquiescence as a result of a number of irreconcilable differences.'

The High Court judge decided that the first of those 'irreconcilable differences' was that Sisu no longer wished to pay as much as they had originally suggested after deciding the shares were not worth that much.

Secondly, the charity's trustees had concerns over a lack of security for the £4.5m of payments which had been promised over the next ten years – and Sisu were not prepared to offer any.

Finally, the judge decided that the charity was not seriously interested in pursuing the £5.5m deal in the original term sheet after August 2012 because they knew that the council was not prepared to consent to it, and was pursuing an alternative strategy which they supported.

Sisu were clearly angry about that alternative deal being discussed between the charity and the council.

The legal team representing the club's owners levelled some strong allegations against the conduct of the charity's trustees as they labelled the deal discussed with the council 'secret and perverse'.

But Mr Leggatt came to the defence of the charity in his judgment.

He said: 'The criticisms made of the Trustees by Sisu as to the propriety of their conduct in December [2012] and January [2013] and the arguments made about them undermining the bargain by their actions at that time are misplaced, and it is unfortunate that allegations were made in some of the pejorative terms which have been used by Sisu in these proceedings.

'There was no warrant for those allegations.'

It was also difficult to take Sisu's complaint seriously when the court also heard they used property firm CBRE to approach Yorkshire Bank behind the backs of the council and the charity at around the same time.

However, there could be little doubt that key figures within the council were far from Sisu's biggest fans and they were clearly opposed to a deal for the charity's shares towards the end of negotiations. In August 2012, an internal memorandum from Chris West, the head of legal and finance at Coventry City Council, was sent to Martin Reeves, the council's chief executive.

In that memorandum, it was made clear that there was opposition within the council to any deal being done with Sisu. They also talked about the alternative scheme, which we will cover in the next chapter.

Moving on for now, the value of the charity's shares in ACL was clearly a bone of contention.

The charity and Sisu signed an outline agreement for the half-share in ACL for £1.5m up front and £4m in shares in the stadium company, which it could cash in at a later date.

But after looking at the books, Sisu said they actually believed the share was worthless. Yet, bizarrely, in separate informal discussions later in the year, they still said they would be willing to pay close to £2m for it.

However, the parties were clearly poles apart. One document read out in court demonstated that the Higgs Charity trustees valued the charity's shares in ACL at closer to £7.5m – so in their eyes £5.5m was already a big discount. There was also clearly the desire to see a return on the charity's original £6.5m investment when it purchased the shares in 2003.

The £2m figure emerged as the court heard evidence that the charity also pursued an alternative deal for Sisu to purchase the Higgs share in ACL away from negotiations about Sisu taking on ACL's debt from Yorkshire Bank.

Higgs Charity trustee Paul Harris was the one who initially gave evidence suggesting this offer was in the region of £2m.

Two communications between Paul Harris and Sisu (or the club on Sisu's behalf) in October and November 2012 gave some insight into how serious those discussions actually were.

In October, Paul Harris had a breakfast meeting with Joy Seppala when she stated that Sisu remained interested in acquiring the charity's interest in ACL but, given the due diligence on ACL, she said that the figure was likely to be closer to £2m rather than the £5.5m figure in the indicative term sheet.

Paul Harris responded that he was sure the trustees would not be interested in such a transaction, even if the offer was in cash.

From that point on, he had no further direct discussion with Joy Seppala.

However, on 10 November 2012, he received three text messages from Tim Fisher, asking him whether he had spoken further to Joy Seppala.

In the third of those messages, Tim Fisher said: 'I was clear that you would sit on the position if the price was not right. Equally, Joy is clear that although equity is worth zero, there is a price to pay. Horse trading now.'

Paul Harris did not respond to that text message. When asked in court about the position at that time, Paul Harris said that from his point of view, and that of the trustees, there was at this stage no longer any reasonable prospect of a deal being done.

Laura Deering, an adviser to Sisu boss Joy Seppala, confirmed the £2m figure and told the court the offer was significantly less than the £5.5m due to the increased risk to Sisu and because the charity wanted 'cash up front'.

Under questioning from Higgs' barrister Paul Brennan, Laura Deering said: 'Mr Harris had asked for a deal to be done with the charity apart from the deal with the council and the bank debt.

'The reduction in the purchase price was because of the risk we would be taking on. We would effectively be buying the Higgs Charity share away from the moving parts.

'Mr Harris suggested that cash could be paid up front apart from the other transaction.

'She [Joy Seppala] recognised that the company [ACL] was worth nothing.'

Asked by Paul Brennan why Joy Seppala was willing to pay £2m for a share that they thought was worth nothing, Ms Deering said: 'She recognised they were a charity.'

Paul Brennan asked if Joy Seppala could be considered 'a sentimental person' and pushed for more details as to why she would be willing to pay a seven-figure sum for something she thought was worthless.

Laura Deering added: 'She recognised the value of what the charity had given.'

She also said that, while the charity had no legal obligation to continue negotiations with Sisu in good faith, it had a moral obligation to do so due to the fact the company had continued to fund Coventry City on the basis of a deal being done.

This was an important point from Sisu's perspective because the owners claimed the club was close to liquidation in 2012 and they saw a reduced rent and stadium ownership deal as a possible way of avoiding winding the business up.

Chief executive Tim Fisher is quoted in Sisu's legal documents as saying that the club would file for insolvency if a stadium deal wasn't reached.

It was clear the club was struggling and most people can agree the £1.3m rent was way too high for a club in Coventry City's predicament.

The club claimed average rents in League One were less than £170,000-a-year in 2012 and less than £290,000 in the Championship. It also claimed all other clubs which rent their stadia get full access to 100 per cent of matchday food, beverage and car parking revenues, unlike Coventry [thanks to their lease arrangement with ACL].

They also claimed ACL was close to insolvency at this point – hence why they reached the conclusion that the Higgs Charity's shares in the Ricoh Arena firm were worthless.

It was a message pushed publicly by Tim Fisher again when speaking on BBC radio in June 2013.

He said: 'Now, when we started the due diligence, we got into the numbers and we drilled down, we realised the business was nothing short of appalling, so actually there is no real business there.

'Half of something very small is very, very small and if you think the football club is struggling, I will tell you ACL is likely struggling and this is the point: two turkeys don't an eagle make.

'We would not strap ourselves to an ailing business and that is why we have to create our own.'

The club not paying its originally agreed rent had clearly made the business weak and other evidence was presented which showed the business could do a lot better.

But Sisu's own document outlining their case quoted Yorkshire Bank, which had the loan to ACL, as saying: 'With appropriate cost savings, a solvent debt restructuring could be agreed.'

In other words, it would appear that the bank thought the company could carry on in business and pay off its loan.

But this was early in 2012 – and we subsequently learned that, as time went on without the club paying the £1.3m agreed rent, ACL's financial difficulties would become critical. It subsequently emerged that, without an anchor tenant, it wouldn't be able to wash its face.

The rent issue was a big one, and one that would have disastrous effects for the club in the coming months. Perhaps only those directly involved in conversations at that time will truly know what was and wasn't agreed – but one piece of communication from 2012 which did become public came from the charity's Peter Knatchbull-Hugessen.

He wrote to Tim Fisher on 11 March 2012, making it clear that City failing to pay rent was a non-starter and demanding guarantees of funding for the club before any sale of the charity's stake in ACL.

Sisu argued that they had continued to make ongoing 'pay as you play' payments to ACL during 2012 – payments which eventually totalled in the region of £230,000 for the 12 months the club was not paying the agreed rent.

Sisu lawyers have also argued that ACL also received £750,000 from the club in escrow [money kept by a third party and released only when specified conditions have been fulfilled] payments between August and December 2012.

Those escrow payments came after the club was taken to court by ACL in August over the unpaid rent.

At the time of the August legal proceedings, Tim Fisher said: 'I can confirm that there is a legal process currently being followed.

'The ACL board of directors are required to follow this process to satisfy their fiduciary responsibilities and duties.

'It is absolutely correct that the ACL directors act in a fit and proper manner.

'During our on-going rent negotiations to date, there have been no twists, turns or surprises.

'It has been a straightforward financial negotiation.

'The board of Coventry City has been kept fully informed by ACL of all developments – legal or otherwise – at all times.

'It is our expectation that the discussions will be concluded before the start of the season.

'Both sides are confident that we will reach an agreement on a rental structure that is fair and reasonable and reflects the interests of both Coventry City and ACL.'

But by December, and after ten months of negotiations, the atmosphere had changed. No solution had been found over the rent, and ACL said it was now owed £1.1m.

That prompted ACL to issue a statuary demand to the owners of the football club, giving them 21 days to settle the debt or face a winding-up order.

The rent row had reached a critical point – and the club had until Boxing Day to find a solution. Not the ideal Christmas present.

An ACL statement at the time read: 'The board feels that all other avenues to resolve this issue have been exhausted and is astonished that the club's owners have allowed matters to come to this sorry pass.

'Responsibility for this situation lies completely with Sisu, a Mayfair hedge fund which has let CCFC fail under its direction.'

But Jacky Isaac, ACL's interim chief executive, told the *Coventry Telegraph* the company could survive without the football club.

She said: 'We would like them to pay but we are a strong business and football is a tiny part of what we do. We are a strong, ongoing business.

'We'd rather have the football club playing here but, yes, it can survive.

'We would like them to be playing here and it is very sad we have had to do this, but it is down to Sisu.

'I used to work at the club and I feel very sad for all the people who work for the club. I feel genuinely sad for the fans and the people at the club.

'We would like to reach a negotiated settlement and have the club playing here.'

Coventry City's statement in response made a startling claim that few could take seriously at the time. It was the first public indication that the club might look to move into an alternative ground. But that would never happen... would it?

The club statement read: 'While we have been seeking to normalise the rent, we have continued to pay matchday costs to ensure that ACL is not left out of pocket.

'These costs amount to over £250,000 per season, much more than the average rent paid by League One clubs.

'The club remains committed to the city and people of Coventry. However, its viability depends on it finding an alternative home ground where it can afford to play.'

Chapter Seven

Keeping council

BY the end of December 2012, the relationship between the club and its owners with the Higgs Charity and Coventry City Council was almost completely broken. Almost a year of negotiations had produced no new rent deal, and the club was seemingly as far away as ever from securing a share in the Ricoh Arena.

On one hand, there was a profit-driven hedge fund with negotiations being led by no-nonsense investment bankers. They are trying to find common ground with a not-for-profit charity, led by individuals who have pledged to act selflessly to improve the city and the life of its people.

Then, just to add another ingredient to the cocktail of chaos we have the public sector in the shape of Coventry City Council, a local authority led by public servants tying themselves in knots and red tape while dedicating huge amounts of time and energy to the bureaucracy associated with making sure they act appropriately.

So we have the private sector, the public sector, the third sector and we need them to work together and come to mutually beneficial agreements. As you can imagine, this is a challenge at the best of times – and is almost impossible when the relationship appears to already have disintegrated. On 10 December 2012, a meeting was held between Sisu, ACL and Coventry City Council to try to find a solution to the stadium ownership and rent issues.

Importantly, at this time, the council was conducting parallel negotiations with Yorkshire Bank about buying out ACL's loan itself – of which about £15.25m still needed to be paid.

Sisu insists it did not know that the council was pursuing this deal with Yorkshire Bank.

On 17 December, Yorkshire Bank indicated to the council that they were unwilling to settle the loan at a reduced level. They believed it could be repaid in full subject to ACL being restructured.

But by 21 December, that stance had changed and the bank agreed to sell the loan to Coventry City Council for £14m having previously rejected offers of £6m and £12m.

The council's decision to purchase the debt and authorise a new £14.4m loan from the local authority to ACL was agreed unanimously by councillors during a private vote on 15 January.

Sisu insists this was a deliberately orchestrated 'perverse and secret' attempt by the city council to scupper any chance of the football club ever owning a stake in the Ricoh Arena. The hedge fund insists the council was trying to force them out as owners of the club and that the deal the council struck with Yorkshire Bank and ACL was unlawful. They say that no rational commercial lender would have agreed to make that loan on the same terms and that it amounted to 'state aid'. They complain that it was an agreement motivated by malice from the council towards Sisu.

It was also argued that Sisu's original offer to buy out the debt was clearly a better option and in the best interests of taxpayers. They also argued they could not afford to continue to pay the £1.3m annual rent – and most parties seemed to agree that a compromise needed to be found in this area.

The council, however, argues that it acted entirely within European state aid regulations. It says it had to act to protect its investment in ACL which was under threat as a direct result of the club's rent strike.

They say Sisu's offer was not better because it was based on securing the Yorkshire Bank debt at an unrealistically low level.

Sisu made the decision to challenge the loan agreement in court via a judicial review. That meant an extremely intelligent and highly qualified judge by the name of Lord Justice Hickinbottom had the pleasure of poring through the evidence during a three-day High Court hearing held at Birmingham High Court in June 2013.

He subsequently reached a judgment which has since been upheld by three senior law lords at the Court of Appeal. At the time of writing, the judgement had been sent to the Supreme Court by the football club's owners – but not before the three law lords praised the original judgement from judge Hickinbottom as 'impressive'.

The key aspects of the arguments from both sides, as covered by the informed legal mind of Judge Hickinbottom, warrant closer inspection.

Sisu claimed that they knew nothing of Coventry City Council's plan to buy out Yorkshire Bank's debt. The judge said he did not believe this to be the case because the bank had appointed Deloitte to look at ACL's cash flow and consider future lending options and that the organisation had contacted Sisu in November 2012 – before the council loan was agreed in January.

Judge Hickinbottom said: 'As part of their investigations, in November, Deloitte met Sisu; so that, from then, Sisu were aware that the council was making its own attempt to purchase the bank debt.

'Mr [Chris] West [the council's finance director] gave the council cabinet an update on 14 November, and told them that it must be assumed, "Sisu know all."'

One thing all sides did seem to agree on was that the level of rent was too high. At £1.3m a year, it was obvious a third tier level football club would struggle to meet payments of over £100,000 a month.

But evidence heard in court gave some interesting context to the rent figure.

In his judgment, Mr Hickinbottom said the rent spending totalled less than ten per cent of the club's annual outgoings.

He said: 'The football club had been seriously mismanaged. By April 2012, it was in a truly parlous state. CCFC was balance sheet insolvent, incurring regular substantial annual losses, and a loss of £5m on the annual turnover of £10m in 2011/12.

'The contractual rent and licence fee for the Arena of £1.3m per year was significant, but less than ten per cent of total expenditure.

'Relegation to League Division One [*sic*] and the introduction of the financial fair play rules compounded these difficulties.'

The key part of this judicial review was Sisu's claim that the council's loan was 'unlawful' and amounted to illegal state aid.

Much argument was had over the value of ACL and its business performance in the run-up to the council's loan deal. Various valuations of the ACL business were produced, including a valuation scale from financial experts PriceWaterHouseCoopers (PWC) which took into account varying levels of rent from the club.

At March 2011, it valued the Arena with no rent at £6.4m, with a rental of £200,000 at £8.6m, and with a rental of £400,000 at £10.8m.

The PWC report also said that these figures 'could be discounted by up to 30 per cent in an insolvency scenario'.

It said that a commercial loan would typically be 60 to 65 per cent loan to value, at a rate of five per cent or above and an average of seven to ten years repayment period.

The January 2013 Coventry City Council loan to ACL was for £14.4m and would be repaid over 40 years.

It was set at a rate of five per cent per annum for the first five years, and could then be altered at the discretion of the council. But it could not be altered to less than five per cent – or more than two per cent – above the interest rate at which the council could borrow money.

The annual repayments amounted to approximately £800,000, compared with the £1.6m ACL had been paying and the £1.3m they would have paid under the bank's restructuring proposal.

So, at first glance, you can see the council's loan rate seems to be incredibly generous – and perhaps risky deal bearing in mind ACL's uncertain financial performance.

Sisu also questioned the legal advice given to councillors ahead of the decision to vote on the loan, suggesting a report by councillor officer Barry Hastie had been misleading and overestimated the potential for ACL to pay back the council loan. That criticism was later labelled as 'unfounded' by Justice Hickinbottom, who also said the report was 'to be commended' .

The judge ultimately decided the loan was reasonable to make and in line with European state aid laws because there were other important factors to consider – not least the fact that the local authority was a partner in ACL.

Justice Hickinbottom said: 'I must compare the council's action in making the loan on the terms that it did with a hypothetical private market economy investor with the same characteristics as the council. Those notably include the fact that the council was not a new investor: it was also a 50 per cent shareholder in ACL.

'Much of the evidence [including the PwC Report] concerns the criteria by which a new investor would or may have made a loan to ACL in January 2013.

'I have little doubt that a new investor would not have made a £14.4m loan to ACL on the terms that the council did, but that is not the question that I have to consider, which is whether a private market economy operator, with a 50 per cent shareholding in ACL, would have effectively restructured its business by making a £14.4m loan to ACL on the terms that the council made the loan.'

Another issue raised by Sisu was that they believed they could have secured a better deal than the council when buying out the Yorkshire Bank loan.

We know Sisu had secretly approached Yorkshire Bank about taking on the ACL loan away from talks with Coventry City Council and the Higgs Charity in 2011. As previously mentioned, that seems to somewhat undermine Sisu's argument that the council had acted inappropriately by discussing a deal with the bank in private itself.

But, despite there being little evidence of progress made with the bank, Sisu remained adamant that they would have secured a better deal than the council ultimately did when they bought out the remaining £15.25m of the Yorkshire Bank loan for £14m.

It appears Sisu thought they could negotiate the bank down to sell the loan for between £2m and £5m.

Coventry City Council QC James Goudie appeared to poke fun at Sisu for this assumption in the High Court when he said the hedge fund had approached this case as if they were the only viable option available to the council.

He said: 'Sisu may believe that they are God's gift to Coventry, but others are entitled to be sceptical and to form their own opinions.'

Judge Hickinbottom seemed to agree that the alternative Sisu put forward seemed doomed to fail. He said: 'Sisu considered that they may have been able to purchase the ACL debt – for which the bank was exposed to the tune of £19m – for perhaps as low as £2m, but no more than £5m.

On the other hand, the bank were satisfied that ACL could in fact service the entire debt, albeit restructured, and were not prepared to accept any figure in that area.

'The bank appears to have considered that ACL could service a restructured loan of at least £15m, and that the debt was worth more than £12m.

'The bank had not made any provision for any of the debt. In the circumstances, it is inconceivable that the bank would have accepted an offer to purchase the debt for £5m.

'In considering the bank would [or might] accept an offer of £2m to £5m for the debt, Sisu had entirely unrealistic expectations.

'They were not prepared to offer more. Thus, this element of Sisu's plan, too, was doomed to fail.'

Now we move on to the thorny issue of the club's decision to withhold the legally agreed £1.3m rent.

The owners of the club have previously been very touchy about this being referred to as a 'rent strike' and even instructed lawyers to send legal letters to then British Sports Journalist of the Year, David Conn, for use of the term in an article for *The Guardian*. Coventry City's largest supporters group, the Sky Blue Trust, was also on the receiving end of one of these letters simply for linking to that article.

But, anyway, it turns out Mr Conn was right to use the term after the withdrawal of rent by the club was categorically defined as a rent strike by senior High Court judge Justice Hickinbottom in his judgment.

The judge's assessment of what had gone on during 2012 didn't stop there. His judgement was utterly damning of the football club owners' conduct – and perhaps goes some way to explaining why it has been dragged, unsuccessfully, through the Court of Appeal and (at the time of writing) is heading to the Supreme Court. It is, therefore, understandable that the hedge fund would seek to protect its damaged reputation in this way.

During 2012, council officials believed Sisu wished to obtain an interest in (if not control over) ACL and thus the Arena, cheaply and at the council's expense, by purchasing the Higgs Charity share of ACL and the company's Yorkshire

Bank loan. They believed Sisu were deliberately distressing ACL to drive down the value and price of that share and that debt.

Judge Hickinbottom made it plain that ACL had been a viable business up until the club withdrew the £1.3m annual rent. He also said that this had been a conscious strategy by the club's owners.

He said: 'In April 2012, the crisis in ACL was triggered by CCFC/Sisu refusing to pay rent which CCFC was legally obliged to pay, in pursuit of the Sisu strategy to obtain a return on their investment by buying into ACL cheaply. Sisu took that action quite deliberately to distress ACL's financial position, with a view to driving down the value of ACL and thus the price of a share in it, which they coveted.

'Indeed, as I have indicated, in these proceedings, the claimants use the argument that ACL's impending insolvency [which Sisu provoked] drove the value of ACL down by up to 30 per cent. Those were commercial decisions that Sisu were entitled to take.'

Sisu have always argued that it is unfair to say they did not pay rent during the 2012 stand-off, arguing they contributed £500,000 which had been withdrawn from an escrow rent guarantee fund and went on to make further payments of £10,000 a game.

But the judge was not satisfied by this argument. He said: 'No rent had been paid since April 2012, and it is recited that the escrow account of £500,000 had been exhausted in August 2012.

'No rent having been paid, a judgment for it had been obtained and [by the time of the Hastie Report] a statutory notice served. The next step would be for a winding-up petition to be served, with the likely result that CCFC would enter insolvency proceedings.

'That precis cannot be faulted. It refers to the escrow account being used, and the £10,000 per match was not an "interim rent agreement". It was a payment in respect of expenses. It is true that such expenses had not been payable in addition to rent whilst contractual rent was being paid, but that rent was not being paid.'

During the subsequent appeal into the High Court judgment, Sisu tried to push an allegation that the council and/or ACL had actually encouraged them to withhold the rent and deliberately weaken ACL's position.

They said the council had suggested it might be beneficial as talks continued to reduce the price Yorkshire Bank would request to buy out the ACL loan.

It has to be said that this is not entirely beyond the realms of possibility. Certainly the rent strike, and the impact on ACL's business performance, would not have hindered negotiations with the bank, who faced being hit hard if ACL went bust.

But the Court of Appeal judges were far from impressed by the argument.

Sisu QC Rhodri Thompson said the tone of the 2014 High Court judgement was hostile to Sisu and unfairly suggested Sisu's conduct was 'outrageous'.

He added: 'The suggestion this was some sort of ferocious rent strike needs to be read in context, that the council thought this was a good idea while negotiating with the bank.

'The board of ACL said 'let's go softly softly' on rent negotiations while pursuing the bank deal.

'It was positive to have the rent low, to keep the value low.'

'There was a common interest in driving down the value to negotiate better terms with the bank.

'Sisu's strategy was not to drive down the value of ACL. The strategy was to break what was strangling ACL, the unaffordable debt that ACL had and the unaffordable rent that the club had.'

Justice Tomlinson interrupted the Sisu QC and said the reason for withholding rent was 'irrelevant'.

He added: 'Why are we interested? The fact is the club didn't pay legally required rent and that impacted the value of ACL.

'So what? Why are we interested in all this toing and froing?'

Justice Treacy added: 'The judgment says these were actions Sisu were entitled to take. Commercially, they're perfectly entitled to do that.'

Justice Tomlinson replied: 'This is of extremely limited interest. This seems to have generated a lot of heat at the time, but it's a distraction from the issues.'

Back to the original High Court hearing, and Judge Hickinbottom went on to heavily criticise the historic financial performance of the club and Sisu's attempts to blame their financial woes on ACL and the level of rent it was paying.

He also made it clear that Sisu knew exactly what they were getting into when they purchased the club in 2007.

He said: 'The Sisu company CCFC had incurred substantial losses – regular losses of £4m to £6m per year including, in 2011/12, a £5m loss on a turnover of £10m – and was clearly balance sheet insolvent.

'It appears to be common ground that poor management greatly contributed to these commercial problems of CCFC. Sisu invested about £40m in CCFC until 2012, and, as I understand it, another approximately £10m from April 2012 until CCFC's demise [administration, which we will cover later in the book].

'Sisu now seek to blame these financial woes on the rent for the Arena which they had to pay which, they have been at pains to stress at every opportunity, was considerably higher than CCFC's competitors in the Championship yet alone League Division One [*sic*], but that is to look at only one small part of the whole canvas.

'CCFC had sold their right to revenues from the Arena, to the Higgs Charity for good consideration; when Sisu bought CCFC, they did so in full knowledge of the absence of any right to Arena revenues and CCFC's contractual commitments, including the commitment to pay rent at £1.3m to ACL; and the outgoings on rent were only a relatively small percentage – less than ten per cent – of the football club's expenditure.'

The judge also compared the council's investment to the one Sisu had made themselves in the club.

He said: 'Sisu now seek to show that, in making a £14.4m loan to ACL in which it owned a half-share, the council acted in a way which no rational private investor would act.

'However, they invested perhaps £50m in the hopelessly loss-making football club – £10m after April 2012 – in the speculative hope that they could make profits in the future, by buying into the Arena.'

Coventry City Council argued that the £14.4m loan it made to ACL was necessary in order to protect its investment in the stadium. But Mr Goudie dismissed that option – pointing to the fact the council was a 50 per cent shareholder in the firm along with The Higgs Charity.

He said: 'Sisu's conduct does come into equation. In fact, it takes centre stage. It represented a threat to the council's commercial interest that could not be ignored.

'Up to the rent strike, ACL was profitable. A consequence of the rent strike was to place the council in circumstances it could not ignore.

'What could they have done instead that would have been a lesser commercial evil? That's where Sisu's case totally breaks down.'

He added: 'The council could not itself put ACL into liquidation, because of the bank's overriding power. It could have stood by and let that happen, but that would have been an extreme solution.

'A public body would have allowed a company it and a charity had a 50 per cent stake in to go insolvent.

'That argument doesn't stack up. It's not only deeply unpalatable, it's plainly wrong.'

Mr Goudie also added that allowing ACL to go bust would have caused damage to the council's commercial reputation, and that was an important consideration in the long term.

The argument that allowing ACL to go bust was a better commercial option for the council was dismissed initially in the Court of Appeal when Judge Hickinbottom said: 'On the basis of all the evidence, in my judgement, a rational private market operator in the position of the council might well have considered that refinancing ACL on the terms in fact agreed was commercially preferable to allowing ACL to become insolvent.'

That view was later backed up by the Court of Appeal when Lord Justice Tomlinson ruled: 'The circumstances that Sisu's plan to buy out the bank debt had irretrievably run aground perhaps demonstrates that there was no viable alternative to the CCC plan, other than perhaps allowing ACL to go into insolvent liquidation, an alternative which the judge convincingly found the council was entitled to reject.'

The football club's owners, on many occasions, suggested the bail-out of ACL in January 2013 had been done behind their backs. As we covered previously, there was a suggestion that Sisu actually knew about the council plan to take over the ACL loan. People will have to make their own decision on what the situation was in reality.

Regardless, Sisu strongly asserted the £14.4m loan to ACL was strongly motivated by a desire within the council to stop Sisu securing a stake in ACL and potentially force them out of the club.

There is evidence that there was ill feeling towards Sisu within the council. There is also strong evidence that ACL and the council believed they could force Sisu out as owners of the club through the administration process (which is covered later).

Internal council memos cited a distrust of Sisu, and one informal note taken during a council meeting in August appeared to suggest at least one member of the authority thought they should only do a deal for the Ricoh Arena with the hedge fund 'when hell freezes over'.

That same note also asked 'could Sisu sell on to another shyster?', which clearly implied the author thought Sisu might seek to move on if they were unsuccessful in securing a share in the Arena.

There appears to be little doubt that those locked in disputes with Sisu would rather someone else ran the city's football club. But why wouldn't there be opposition to Sisu if these officials believed the hedge fund was trying to destroy a business which the council owned in partnership with a local charity?

A potential conflict of interest was also raised by Sisu's legal team with Coventry City Council chief executive Martin Reeves and finance chief Chris West, both also appearing on the board of directors for ACL. Sisu suggested the pair could have had undue influence over the council's decision to allow the loan to ACL. But the judge later said the advice provided to councillors by officers was satisfactory and even praised the thoroughness of the financial reports.

In summary, it's almost certain there was animosity within the council towards Sisu at the time, but the courts were not impressed by the emphasis placed on this by the hedge fund's QC.

Justice Hickinbottom branded it as irrelevant, suggesting Sisu was never in a position to agree a deal for a stake in ACL.

Justice Hickinbottom said: 'The council do not accept that its officers acted in a manner "calculated fundamentally to undermine" the Sisu negotiations.

'But, in any event, as I have explained, the Sisu plan had terminally stalled by the end of August 2012, because it was impossible for them to agree to purchase the Higgs Charity share in ACL, which was vital to the plan as a whole. This ceased being a material consideration well before January 2013.'

The Court of Appeal went further and labelled it a distraction from the real issues in its judgment.

Lord Tomlinson said: 'I found merely distracting the appellant's emphasis upon the apparent animosity towards Sisu manifested by some in the controlling group on the council.

'I found equally irrelevant the council's apparent belief, or at any rate the belief of some on the council, that Sisu had behaved in an unacceptable or predatory manner.'

He added: 'Even if one accepts that some councillors wanted nothing to do with Sisu, and puts to one side the fact the decision of the council was in fact unanimous, still the focus of the enquiry is whether the transaction was one that could have been entered into by a market economy operator.'

The issue of how terribly Sisu believed they had been treated by the council emerged again during a Coventry City Council ethics committee hearing held over two days and concluded in January 2016. That committee ruled there had been no breach of the council's code of conduct by Cllr John Mutton, who was leader of the council leading up to and at the time of the bail-out, and then council leader Ann Lucas.

Unsurprisingly perhaps, the result was branded a 'whitewash' by Sisu. But it did allow the hedge fund to make some of their grievances with the council public.

The ethics panel, made up of councillors from the Labour and Conservative Party, considered the complaints from Sisu and an independent report into what had occurred by Simon Goacher of law firm Weightmans.

The panel heard allegations that Cllr Mutton had been 'rude' and 'aggressive' towards Sisu boss Joy Seppala during talks with the council about acquiring a 50 per cent stake in the Ricoh Arena operating firm ACL during 2012.

But the author of the independent report, Mr Goacher, said the evidence was not there to back up those claims and questioned the timing of the complaint.

He said: 'If the behaviour was as bad as you now say it was, you wouldn't have waited three years to make a complaint about it.'

Cllr Mutton also dismissed the allegations, referring to one meeting where he and Ms Seppala had hugged and explained it wasn't a one-off example of how they had communicated in the past, in a bid to demonstrate there was no animosity or aggression.

The club owners also said the language used by Cllr Mutton and Cllr Lucas in public statements at the time had been inappropriate and defamatory.

Cllr Mutton was quoted as saying that 'Sisu is a predator with greed running through its DNA' and had also admitted to chanting 'Sisu Out' at one match.

But Cllr Mutton said the first comment was simply him repeating during a BBC radio interview what former Coventry North East MP Bob Ainsworth had said in Parliament.

He added: 'Yes, I did join in the chant [but] it wasn't as a councillor [and] it certainly wasn't as leader of the council.

'It was as someone who has supported the club since seven years of age and was a season ticket holder that had seen the club go downhill rapidly during that time.'

Mr Goacher said Cllr Mutton had been entitled to make the comments because 'what the law strives to achieve is a balance where people are allowed to express themselves in a way which allows robust discussion of matters in the public interest.

'Some of Cllr Mutton's comments get close to the line, I don't think they cross it.'

He added the comments could also be justified as they were personal beliefs rather than gratuitous and personal insults.

As well as the conduct of the senior councillors during the Ricoh Arena discussions, Sisu attempted to suggest there had been a concerted media campaign against the football club and that the council had played an active role in it.

There was a catalogue of extracts from media articles included in Sisu's evidence, which highlighted public comments made by councillors and officials in a bid to back up the argument.

E-mails and briefing documents from London PR firm Weber Shandwick were also read out which suggested targeting Joy Seppala, encouraging journalists to visit her at home and that a 'media war' was being fought. The PR company had been hired by by ACL – the firm which was jointly owned by the council and the Higgs Charity. However, both organisations denied use of the PR company directly and insisted Weber Shandwick was only ever employed by ACL. This distinction is made even more cloudy by the fact senior council officers and Higgs Charity officials sat on the ACL board at this time.

However, there did not seem to be any evidence that the suggestions made by Weber Shandwick were ever actually followed through. On the evidence available, ACL seemed to be paying hefty consultancy fees to a PR firm for advice that was never acted on.

The author of the independent report into the complaint, Simon Goacher, said: 'When you follow the schedule [of e-mails] and what was actually said, it doesn't seem to have been replicated. There's no evidence of that. It isn't translated to press comments to support this is what was going on.'

This allegation of press manipulation was seen as insulting to journalists at media outlets who had covered the Ricoh Arena saga over the years. The implication that a public relations firm is able to control members of the press and railroad them into writing exactly what they want is, in my experience, absurd.

During my time covering the stadium issue, there has certainly been pressure from all sides to present things in a certain way from time to time. But journalists don't tend to crack under pressure.

Some parties resorted to different ways of leaning on journalists. For instance, only Sisu has even resorted to involving solicitors – sometimes over seemingly obscure points – during my time at the *Telegraph*. It has also been my experience that the most pressure over the tone of coverage has undoubtedly come from the Sisu/CCFC side of the argument. During Mark Labovitch's spell on the club's board, I had regular dialogue with him.

That's not to say others didn't apply pressure, of course. However, I can honestly say you could probably count on two hands the amount of times Weber Shandwick, the charity or the council picked up the phone to me to complain about, or attempt to influence, coverage in the *Coventry Telegraph* in relation to the stadium saga.

But wherever the pressure emanated from, it was nothing more than a distraction and it certainly did not influence the way I reported or presented a story at any point. And I would hope none of the reporters at the *Telegraph* covering the stadium saga before I arrived could be bent to the will of any of the parties involved. I can confidently say nobody should question the professionalism of the team at the *Telegraph* today.

At various points throughout the Ricoh Arena saga, allegations of some sort of far-reaching conspiracy to target the club's owners and force them out have surfaced repeatedly – usually when things don't seem to be going so well for Sisu. I'm sure this is just a coincidence and in no way meant to distract from issues such as a lack of a new stadium or court judgments.

Since I joined the *Telegraph* in July 2013, the list of people apparently involved in this elaborate conspiracy theory has grown ever longer. As well as Coventry City Council, The Higgs Charity and ACL, I have also heard supporters group the Sky Blue Trust, elected members of Parliament and even my employers – the *Coventry Telegraph* – accused of colluding against Sisu.

Now I can categorically say that if there is some sort of elaborate conspiracy to 'get Sisu', I have never been forwarded the memo. Bearing in mind the thousands of pages of evidence, private communications and e-mails which have been turned over to the hedge fund after various legal actions, you would think some solid evidence of such a conspiracy might have emerged by now.

Mark Labovitch used to refer to a 'smoking gun' in relation to all this and assured me it would all come out in the wash. I was also told by several supporters that Mr Labovitch had actively pushed this conspiracy line out to supporters when he held a series of intimate meetings during his time at the club.

I was never entirely clear what Mr Labovitch's role in all this was, but it was rare that anything became clearer after a conversation with him.

But, after three years of covering this sorry saga more closely and in greater depth than any other journalist, I'm still waiting to see any solid evidence of this conspiracy.

I'm aware Sisu's legal team released one e-mail which implied that the then *Coventry Telegraph* editor Alun Thorne had sat on the story about the private council vote to loan ACL £14.4m in January 2013.

The e-mail was sent on the morning of the secret ACL loan vote from council chief executive Martin Reeves to his finance director Chris West, Weber Shandwick's Chris Hogwood, Peter Knatchbull-Hugessen and Paul Harris of the Higgs Charity, Liz Cooper and Jacky Isaac at the Ricoh Arena and Fran Collingham, the council's head of communications.

An extract read: 'I had another extremely constructive and honest discussion with the editor of the *CT* this morning – so all good.'

It adds: 'Fran mentioned Alun was relaxed about councillors appearing on radio/TV as long as he gets the story first.'

Now let me say first of all that I was not at the *Coventry Telegraph* at the time of these events in January 2013, so it's difficult for me to say what exactly went on – and those involved will no doubt have their own views.

What I can tell you is that it is absolutely standard industry practice for journalists to be briefed on an impending major story 'off the record' or 'under embargo'. We are often told sensitive information on the basis that we don't run articles until a certain time.

In addition, I am absolutely certain that *Coventry Telegraph* staff can point to instances throughout the Ricoh Arena row timeline where we have sat on stories for all of the parties involved – including the football club.

If we were to breach these confidences, we would be at a competitive disadvantage as the organisations concerned would be unlikely to brief us in this manner again.

Had I been at the *Telegraph* at the time, I would certainly have pushed for the story to be published if I could get it stood up on the record.

Another important piece of context here is that evidence was heard in court that indicated Sisu already knew about the council plan to bail out ACL. Sisu obviously have denied this repeatedly.

If the council had not informed Sisu of their plans, and there was still any chance of a deal for the football club to gain a stake in an arena built for them, then the council's tactics are undoubtedly morally reprehensible.

But I would also ask what would have happened if Sisu had been made aware of the secret vote in advance? Can a hedge fund really take any sort of action to prevent a democratically elected public body making urgent decisions in what they consider to be the best interests of taxpayers?

If we believe Sisu didn't know about the vote, perhaps we could conclude the club's owners might have made an attractive counter offer had they been warned the vote was coming. But nothing had prevented them from doing that before and the tone of negotiations to that point suggested Sisu wasn't willing to buy out the Yorkshire Bank debt at the level the council paid.

In conclusion, it is my opinion that it's absolutely clear that there was animosity towards Sisu from people within ACL, the council and the Higgs Charity.

It seems they didn't want to do a deal with Sisu for a share in the Ricoh Arena. The evidence also seems to suggest the council, the Higgs Charity and ACL would all have preferred the club to have different owners. Indeed, it seems a lot of time and effort was put in to try to ensure new ownership when the club went through the administration process (which we will cover later).

But did Sisu ever really want to do a deal for the Ricoh Arena during this time?

The evidence suggests certainly not on terms the other parties would have found acceptable. In fact, it appears Sisu took an aggressive approach to securing a share in ACL by withholding rent in a bid to pick up a stake in the company on the cheap. That strategy clearly did not pay off.

Sisu clearly still hotly contest the judgments and the findings of two courts and four senior judges. The legal process will continue in the background. But, for now, the evidence seems pretty damning for all the parties involved directly in the failed stadium negotiations.

Chapter Eight

Administration

I T'S early 2013 and we've just entered what will be one of the darkest years in Coventry City Football Club's history. Talks over a reduced rent deal for the football club at the Ricoh Arena have failed and a £14.4m council bail-out deal for Ricoh Arena firm ACL seems to have killed off any hope of the club securing a stake in the stadium.

Now the action, and the accompanying rhetoric, was being dramatically ramped up.

On 15 February 2013, Ricoh Arena bosses gave the club an unwelcome belated Valentine's Day gift when they served 'third party debtor orders' on the club with a view to recouping their rent arrears. The orders entitled ACL to secure any money the club was owed from third parties to pay down the arrears.

At the time that included money due from Huddersfield Town FC, which was set to pay the Sky Blues compensation for manager Mark Robins, who had just jumped ship, and would eventually be replaced by Steven Pressley.

Other money which could be diverted to ACL included a business rates rebate of almost £400,000, which was due to be repaid to the club after a miscalculation meant they had dramatically overpaid the rates to central government for almost a decade.

The debtor order effectively froze the club's bank accounts and meant none of the third parties named in the court document could pay money to the football club with immediate effect and that would not change until a final debt order was issued by a judge – unlikely to be before May. At that point, ACL would be able to obtain the money.

The development came as ACL claimed Sky Blues directors had reneged on an agreement over an improved rent deal two weeks previously.

ACL said the deal included cutting annual rent payments by two-thirds to £400,000; waiving £300,000 of the rent arrears; a long-term deal over repayments and giving more stadium match day revenue, such as from food and drink sales, to the football club. It was a deal that the stadium firm claimed would effectively reduce the £1.3m annual rent package to just £150,000 paid by the club in 'net' total match day costs while the club remains in League One.

An ACL statement released at the time read: 'The board of Arena Coventry Limited (ACL) has today served interim Third Party Debt Orders on Coventry City Football Club following the collapse of talks around future rent and match-day arrangements.

'The orders have been served in respect of the club's bank account, its card payment acceptance service account, its business rates account with Coventry City Council and Huddersfield Town Football Club.

'These orders, which are expected to be made final orders shortly, will then entitle ACL to lawfully collect any monies owed to the club by these third parties.'

Nicholas Carter, ACL chairman, said: 'We don't want to have to resort to such means as obtaining interim third party debt orders.

'But if the club won't agree to the very generous deal on the table and pay what it lawfully owes, we have a duty to our stakeholders to take all the necessary steps to protect ACL's interests.

'It's our responsibility as directors to do all we can to make sure ACL gets paid.'

Then Coventry City Council leader John Mutton said the third party debt order approach was chosen by ACL because issuing a statutory demand for rent payment in full could have tipped the football club into administration or liquidation.

He said: 'Sisu have to get their heads out of the sand and realise they have two choices; a sensible deal and investment in the football club and a new manager and get the team back into the Championship... or they can chuck their lot into a brown paper bag and walk away.'

Martin Reeves, Coventry City Council chief executive and an ACL board member, added: 'By serving this series of interim third party debt orders, the directors are exercising their legal rights while at the same time giving Coventry City Football Club the best possible opportunity, given the circumstances, to continue as a going concern.'

During this period, the football club and its owners remained uncharacteristically quiet, with few public statements. But ACL continued to fill the void, once again issuing strong statements the following day.

They insisted that a new, lower rent deal had been all but agreed the previous month in a meeting attended by senior Coventry City Council and club officials. The firm had also apparently begun to take exception to suggestions that the football club could seek to move away from the Ricoh Arena.

The 'apparent' meeting had taken place at the Ricoh Arena on 29 January 2013 and had been attended by John Clarke, Tim Fisher and Mark Labovitch from the club.

Peter Knatchbull-Hugessen, clerk for the Higgs Charity, said he was also in attendance and revealed some further details about what had gone on.

He said: 'There was a private meeting at the Ricoh Arena in 2013.

'Mark Labovitch and Tim Fisher and John Clarke were there from the football club, along with Sisu's lawyer Alex Carter-Silk. Paul Harris [Higgs Charity] was there and so was I, as well as Martin Reeves [council chief executive] and Christ West [council finance director].

'We worked out a deal on rent, shook hands and agreed it. If they had stuck to that agreement, there was never the need for them to leave the Ricoh Arena.

'But it fell down because Sisu insisted on being given access to full details of the council loan to ACL before they would agree it.'

It later emerged in court that the deal had actually been vetoed by Sisu's top boss Joy Seppala.

Apparently Ms Seppala was not willing to accept any deal that did not include the club obtaining a stake in ACL. The stalemate continued.

Justice Hickinbottom assessed the situation during the judicial review into the council's loan to ACL.

He said: 'After the council had purchased the bank debt, thereby resolving that immediate sticking point, negotiations over rent continued between CCFC and ACL.

'On 29 January 2013, heads of terms were agreed, involving rent at £400,000 from 1 January 2013 with an agreement on arrears taking into account a reduced escrow account sum [which left arrears of about £500,000 to be paid] and an in-principle agreement for CCFC to benefit from match-day food and beverage revenues and ACL paying a larger share of the rates on the Arena.

'The directors of CCFC and ACL representatives shook hands on that, but the deal was rejected on 4 February 2013 by Ms Seppala [who, as described by [Sisu QC] Mr Thompson, "sat at the top of the tree in terms of [Sisu] decision making"] on the basis that she was not prepared to accept any deal that excluded Sisu from holding a stake in ACL.'

ACL issued a statement at the time outlining what they believed had been agreed in principle.

It read: 'The offer set the rent payable by CCFC at £400,000 per annum while the club remains in Football League One.

'It included agreement from ACL to waive more than £300,000 of the £1,347,000 rent arrears, with a generous approach to clearing the balance. It also agreed the principle of ACL matchday revenues benefiting CCFC, and ACL paying a larger share of rates on the stadium.

'Instead of confirming its written acceptance, CCFC then proposed an alternative heads of terms, which bore no relation to that agreed. It demanded the waiver by ACL of all rent arrears claims pre-dating 1 January 2013. It demanded also the withdrawal of the statutory demand for the payment of rent arrears issued by ACL against CCFC on 5 December 2012.

'It was accompanied by an e-mailed statement from Tim Fisher declaring that CCFC has "no option but to build a new venue" and that CCFC's proposals were predicated on playing at the Ricoh Arena for a 'run-off period of three years.'

It added: 'The board of ACL believes that Sisu have no intention of entering into a meaningful dialogue to resolve this issue."

Then ACL chairman Nicholas Carter was clearly riled by the back-and-forth nature of the negotiations.

He said: 'To spend many hours engaging in positive and constructive discussions, leading to a detailed point-by-point discussion of a proposed heads of terms agreement resulting in verbal agreement and handshakes all round, only to then renege when it came to signing the agreement, is truly reprehensible behaviour.

'There's simply no point in continuing these discussions while the club, under Sisu's ownership, continues to behave in this manner.

'We will only be prepared to resume these conversations if John Clarke, Tim Fisher and Mark Labovitch [the Sky Blues board] sign up to the deal to which they agreed. If the club directors can't or won't follow through on the agreement they participated in creating, then we suggest to them that the time has come to consider offering ownership of CCFC to an outside buyer better placed to run the club's financial operations. Make no mistake, now is the time for Sisu to pay up or sell up and get out of Coventry.'

Strong words from ACL, and the first real public indication that senior figures at the Ricoh Arena wanted Sisu to sell the club.

The firm was also claiming Coventry City officials had told them they planned to build their own stadium, but the club was tight-lipped on this suggestion at this time.

It was hard to believe such a plan could even be feasible, especially for a club suffering from the clear financial difficulties Coventry City had at that time.

Things went from bad to worse for the football club and its owners on 13 March 2013 when a dramatic move by Ricoh Arena bosses edged the club closer to administration – and possibly new owners.

ACL applied for an administration order at the High Court after failing to reach an agreement with the club's owners Sisu over more than £1.3m in unpaid rent.

That meant the club was likely to enter administration and an administrator appointed who could look to sell the club.

The picture was further developed when ACL suggested there were already parties interested in taking over the club amid rumours that potential investors had visited the stadium.

Crucially, administration could also mean a ten-point deduction for the League One club – something which would scupper hopes of reaching the play-offs and promotion in the first season after relegation from the Championship.

Speaking at the time, ACL director Chris West, who is also Coventry City Council's finance director, told the *Coventry Telegraph*: 'We believe there are other parties out there that could be interested.'

One of the strongest rumours circulating at this time was that suspended life president Joe Elliott had been spotted with

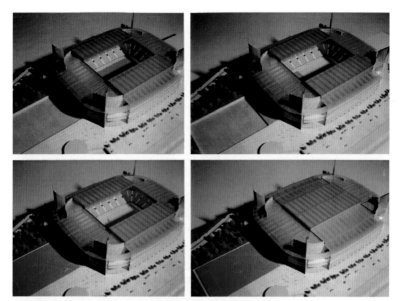
The 'Arena 2000' stadium model pictured in 1997.

Bryan Richardson, CCFC chairman, with the 'Arena 2000' model in January 1999.

Top: The crowd on the Highfield Road pitch following the last game in April 2005. **Middle left:** Andy Whing celebrates scoring the last ever goal at Highfield Road in April 2005. **Middle right:** Fans on the pitch after the last game at Highfield Road in April 2005. **Bottom:** Paul Fletcher, ACL then CCFC managing director, with CCFC chairman Mike McGinnity in 2007.

Top: Geoffrey Robinson (left) with Ray Ranson just a few hours after Sisu had agreed to take over CCFC in December 2007. **Middle:** 'Best board ever' pictured in 2011. (l/r) Paul Clouting, Chief Executive; Ken Dulieu, Chairman; John Clarke, Vice Chairman; Leonard Brody, Director; and Onye Igwe, Director. **Bottom:** Ray Ranson (centre) with Joe Elliott (left) and Gary Hoffman (right) in 2011.

Preston Haskell IV with then Coventry City Council leader John Mutton ahead of the American's CCFC takeover bid in April 2013.

Protesters in Broadgate during the first Sky Blue Trust march in July 2013.

Above: Protesters on Gosford Street first Sky Blue Trust organised march in July 2013.
Right: The *Coventry Telegraph* front page after the club's first game at Sixfields in August 2013.

Coventry Telegraph

MONDAY, AUGUST 12, 2013

Over 7,000 fans watch charity match in Coventry but City's first 'home' game in Northampton is watched by just 2,000

THE RICOH

SIXFIELDS

WE WANT TO GO HOME

Protest at The Emirates during CCFC's FA Cup clash with Arsenal in January 2014.

Protesters fill Broadgate during the second Sky Blue Trust organised protest march in July 2014.

Protesters on the hill at Sixfields in August 2014.

Coventry Telegraph

Friday, August 22, 2014   www.coventrytelegraph.net   55p

After 503 days, 59 games, two marches, 13,000 signatures, a judicial review, six campaigns and thousands of broken hearts, the Sky Blues are finally...

COMING HOME

SEE PAGES 2,3,4,5, 6&7

COVENTRY CITY FOOTBALL CLUB

Above: The *Coventry Telegraph* front page announcing that the Sky Blues would be coming home in August 2014. **Left:** Ray Oliver, Dave Kaczur, George Stringer and Gaz Robinson who were the first group to get their tickets for the Sky Blues' return to the Ricoh Arena in September 2014.

Sisu chief executive Joy Seppala and CCFC chairman Tim Fisher on the Ricoh Arena pitch for CCFC's first game back at the stadium in September 2014.

Steven Pressley and the players return to inspect the Ricoh Arena pitch ahead of their return to the stadium in September 2014.

an American businessman at a Sky Blues home game against Colchester United on a Tuesday night.

The potential American investor was given a tour of the Ricoh Arena by the then ACL interim chief executive Jacky Isaac.

It was later discovered that this mysterious gentleman was Preston Haskell IV, a US property tycoon who had previously expressed an interest in buying Leeds United. The Texan was undoubtedly in a position to make big investments with a fortune estimated at $250m.

Haskell IV is the son of 74-year-old Preston Haskell III, founder of The Haskell Company, the largest privately held construction company in Florida and a top design/build firm in the US.

At the time of being linked to the club, he had recently sold his minority shareholding in NFL team Jacksonville Jaguars.

Haskell IV had moved to Moscow in 1992 to start the Haskell International Group, which began with real estate investment and property management but also operated restaurants and manufactured furniture.

He also had interests in mining in Siberia and Africa, extensive investments in the Democratic Republic of Congo and involvement in a South African vineyard.

Joe Elliott said: 'A week before the club went into administration is when I first met Preston Haskell.

'He came to a night match and liked what he saw and there were many comments from the owners in the press about the financial situation at the club at that time.

'The arrival of Preston Haskell at that time was to me good news. If the club was going to go bust, at least we had someone on hand with cash who could take over.

'I have a lot of contacts around the world with people in investment and football and my introduction to Mr Haskell came through a friend of Gary Hopkins – Gary Otto, a South Africa living in LA.

'I met him at the Westbury Hotel, Mayfair in 2012 and then I didn't hear from him again until 2013, when Gary Otto got in touch with me.'

Ahead of the administration order, club chief executive Tim Fisher had already said in a national newspaper that the club could be heading for administration and insolvent liquidation.

He is quoted as saying: 'They [ACL] need to re-enter negotiations pronto or we file. We'll have no option because there would not be reasonable probability of avoiding insolvency liquidation.'

Those quotes were later backed up by non-executive director Mark Labovitch in the *Coventry Telegraph*.

He said: 'When Tim Fisher mentioned the possibility of administration, this was not a tactic or posturing. It is a matter of the law.

'If a company sees no possibility of avoiding insolvent liquidation, it is legally compelled to go into administration.'

Around this time, Tim Fisher had also publicly mooted the prospect of Sisu building a new stadium and leaving the Ricoh.

ACL's lawyer James Powell said the measure had been taken to stop the club entering liquidation, a move that would have meant a reformed club which would have had to start again after plummeting down the football pyramid. In other words, liquidation would probably mean Coventry City having to reform in the Evostik League Southern.

It would be a similar outcome to the one fans had recently endured at Glasgow Rangers.

ACL director and council finance chief Chris West said the timing of the administration should also allow for a ten-point deduction that season, rather than next season – something he viewed as preferable.

He added: 'We're doing this as [ACL] company directors to protect the interests of the company.

'We want to preserve the Sky Blues and the Sky Blues playing at the Ricoh Arena.

'One of the advantages of this legal action is it prevents the club being liquidated.

'Tim Fisher has openly said this week the club is at a "tipping point and insolvent liquidation cannot be reasonably avoided." It gives us the best possible chance for whoever to come in and re-stabilise the club in the interests of ACL, the football club and the city.'

ACL chairman Nicholas Carter said: 'It is highly unfortunate that we have had to take this course of legal action. Had we not taken this action, then the alternative might have been catastrophic for CCFC.

'We are owed a considerable amount of money in rent arrears. While it is imperative that ACL takes action to recover these arrears and to stop the arrears growing, it is important for us to find a solution that can provide for the survival of the Sky Blues.

'We are, of course, well aware that under the current Football League regulations, CCFC will face a points deduction and we will do everything we can to ensure that the case is heard by the High Court before the end of the current season.

'While this opens up the possibility of a ten-point deduction this season, the board believes this is better than leaving CCFC facing a much larger deduction at the start of next season.'

What would happen during an administration process at Coventry City was explained by Brendan Guilfoyle, who has acted as administrator for numerous professional sports clubs, including Portsmouth FC.

He told the *Coventry Telegraph* that if the club went into administration, the Football League would suspend its 'golden share' or league place.

He added: 'Then, providing the club can exit through a Company Voluntary Arrangement [CVA], the league will restore that share – normally to a new company.

'And the club's league position, subject to sporting sanctions, will be reinstated. I don't want to say 'someone will always come forward', but there are no reasons why there won't be potential purchasers here.'

A CVA is an agreement between an insolvent company and its creditors to pay them back a specified amount within an agreed time period. But it emerged that, in an administration situation, Sisu would have the most power as the single biggest creditor, having invested tens of millions into the club as loans during this period.

Mr Guilfoyle explained this meant Sisu could attempt to block any takeover – but there could be severe consequences.

Mr Guilfoyle said: 'Could Sisu as the largest creditor scupper the CVA by not agreeing to it? Yes, they could. But that doesn't mean the administrator couldn't sell the club.

'There is a precedent with Leeds United whereby they couldn't get the CVA through, so the new owners applied to transfer the club in 'special circumstances.'

'But in doing so, the Football League gave the club a second 15-point deduction. But I don't know whether it will come to that with Coventry City.'

With fears over the future of Coventry City dominating talk on the terraces, the club's chief executive Tim Fisher sought to deflect blame on to the stadium operators.

He said: 'We have not applied for a court application, which could send the club into administration.

'That has been done to us.

'There is no benefit to the football club, its supporters or any other party to discuss financial and commercial details through the media. Why would we do that when we are at such a delicate stage in proceedings?

'We are doing everything we can to work through this while at the same time running a football club that is doing very well on the field and in touching distance of the play-off places.'

On 21 March 2013, Coventry City's owners took control of the situation when the club's single biggest creditor – Sisu company Arvo – placed Coventry City Football Club Limited into administration. The owners then subsequently appointed their own administrator, Paul Appleton, of insolvency specialists David Rubin. ACL unsuccessfully challenged this move in court, preferring instead to appoint their own administrator in the shape of Mr Guilfoyle.

The administration triggered an immediate problem for the Sky Blues. They had three home games left to play, but their agreement to use the stadium had now effectively ceased to exist.

Frantic conversations were held as the club investigated possibilities which would allow it to complete the season – including playing at alternative venues.

But ACL insisted they had no intention of forcing the club elsewhere for the rest of the season. Tim Fisher immediately moved to reassure fans with a statement suggesting a short-term deal would likely be agreed for the League One fixtures against Doncaster Rovers, Brentford and Leyton Orient.

He said: 'The long-term licence was terminated by the administrator, but we are hopeful that Coventry City Football Club [Holdings] Ltd can reach agreement with ACL to allow the team to play its final three games of the season at the Ricoh.

'We appreciate that our supporters have been through a great deal of upset and uncertainty, and there is a responsibility on all parties to ensure that the question of where we play our remaining three home games is resolved as soon as possible.

'Allowing supporters to watch the Sky Blues at the Ricoh for three games would be a sensible step forward. We have contacted ACL and hope to have some clarity in the next 24 hours.'

The distinction in that statement of Coventry City Football Club (Holdings) sticks out like a sore thumb. But there's a reason why it was worded this way.

Coventry City officials sought to avoid any penalty from the Football League by insisting the golden share was actually in Coventry City Football Club (Holdings) and that CCFC Ltd has merely been a non-operating property subsidiary.

A statement from the club at the time said: 'It is important to stress that the football club itself is not under threat.

'This is merely a property subsidiary which owns no material assets and has no employees, on or off the pitch.

'The club can confirm that all staff wages, PAYE and all other creditor commitments will continue to be met as before by Coventry City Football Club [Holdings].

'Unlike other instances of clubs being taken either wholly or partially into administration, there are no HMRC or VAT implications and the football club will continue to trade as normal without interruption.

'Our main objective now is to remain competitive on the pitch and give Steven Pressley and the playing staff our full backing and commitment.'

The hunt for the golden share was on and clearly there was a difference of opinion over where it was hiding. Sisu insisted it sat in CCFC (Holdings) – the firm still owned by its Cayman Islands hedge fund Arvo and not in administration, while ACL claimed it was in CCFC Ltd – the company in administration.

ACL lawyer James Powell said: 'We had a letter from the Football League confirming the share is with Coventry City FC Ltd. The FA also confirmed the FA share is with Coventry City FC Ltd.

'That company is in administration, with an administrator appointed by Joy Seppala.

'We held off our application for a few days to get to the bottom of key issues, including Football League shares.

'There were inconsistencies in statements from the club. It's clear to us the whole club is in administration.

'Coventry City FC Ltd is not a non-operating subsidiary, as the club claims. The club exists where Football League and FA shares rest, with CCFC Ltd.'

Why ACL were so keen to insist the share was in one company rather than the other would later become clear. The stadium firm hoped the administration process would allow new owners to swoop in and oust Sisu. New owners were only likely to be attracted if they were certain they could obtain the Football League share.

Off-the-pitch events were no longer just an unhelpful distraction. The fall-out was likely to have a very real impact on City's play-off hopes with a points deduction looming. Furthermore, the club did not know where it would be playing its final home games that season.

Just over 24 hours before the Sky Blues were due to line up at home to league leaders Doncaster Rovers, the players, supporters and managers did not know where the game would be played. It was a farcical situation.

Manager Steven Pressley told the *Coventry Telegraph* all he could do was continue to work on the premise that the play-offs remained an option.

He said: 'It's a pivotal weekend. This will decide whether or not we have an opportunity for the play-offs or not.

'There's a great willingness from them to do well for the football club and we'll work towards that and the players will be giving everything they can to ensure we stay in contention.'

He added: 'I think it's the ideal scenario to play the remaining home games at the Ricoh and beyond that it's down to the various parties to find a solution. But I think between now and the end of the season, from a football department point of view, that would be the ideal solution.'

With just hours to go until the crunch game, a deal was struck for the club to play its last three games at the Ricoh Arena. A strange joint statement from the administrator and ACL confirmed the news.

It read: 'Paul Appleton, Joint Administrator for Coventry City FC Ltd, and Arena Coventry Ltd are pleased to confirm a deal has been agreed which allows the Club to play the final three home fixtures of the season at the Ricoh Arena.'

A statement from the club read: 'Coventry City Football Club Holdings Ltd are pleased that an agreement has been reached with ACL and the Administrator that enables us to play our last three remaining home matches at the Ricoh Arena. We apologise profusely to our fans about the confusion surrounding these fixtures and are delighted that this has now been resolved.

'We can now look forward to playing current league leaders Doncaster in the hope of doing the double over them.

'Moving forward, we hope that we can continue a constructive dialogue with ACL with the aim of securing a sustainable future for the club at the Ricoh Arena.'

But it appeared the Football League was unimpressed by the continuing attempts to distinguish CCFC Ltd from CCFC Holdings. Just hours after the announcement that the Sky Blues would be able to finish the season, the league finally extinguished any lingering promotion hopes.

A ten point deduction was imposed, killing off the Sky Blues' play-off ambitions.

A brief statement from the Football League read: 'The Football League can confirm that Coventry City Football Club have been deducted ten points, in accordance with its rules and regulations.

'This sporting sanction has been implemented with immediate effect and the Sky Blues have seven days in which to appeal.

'The League has now begun discussions with the administrator aimed at achieving a sustainable future for the club within the Football League.'

CCFC's owners did appeal, but it was ultimately unsuccessful.

The issues were not just affecting the first team either. The administration of CCFC Ltd had meant the academy had not been able to pay its bills for use of the Alan Edward Higgs Centre and therefore had been told they were no longer able to use the facilities. The row escalated, primarily over the £12,000 costs of repairing a lawnmower used to maintain the pitches at the Allard Way site.

By the summer, office equipment had been removed and club signage taken down, and the academy's players moved to train at the club's Ryton training base.

Peter Knatchbull-Hugessen launched a scathing attack on the club's owners at the time over the issue.

He said: 'They got the grass pitches for nothing but they had to maintain them and they used our equipment to do that. These mowers are very expensive bits of kit and the capital cost of the equipment there was £100,000.

'They paid rent for the offices and the all-weather pitches. They paid a discounted rate because they paid quarterly in advance.

'It couldn't have been better for them. There's no capital recovery, no fee for use of pitches and it would have cost them more if they owned it.

'They wouldn't pay for pitch renovation, so they consume and use and don't pay, and as a charity, which is what The Higgs is, that can't go on.

'I don't understand; presumably they know what they are doing.'

Steve Waggott, then the club's development director, moved to reassure fans.

He said: 'Nobody should underestimate just how important the academy is to Coventry City Football Club and our future plans are geared towards identifying the best possible talent and developing it through our system.

'This is something that has required strong investment in terms of time and money but, again, is vital to the future of the football club.'

Events away from football continued, and administrator Paul Appleton announced his findings in a report issued on 15 May.

Figures in the report showed Sisu firm Arvo was owed more than £10m.

It also calculated that ACL was actually owed a 'net liability' of £600,000 at the start of the year, after taking into account that ACL had removed £500,000 from a rent deposit account.

At that point, fees for the administrator had already reached £163,294 plus VAT for 475 hours' work since his appointment. The administrator's solicitors, Stephenson Harwood LLP, had incurred another £143,646 costs plus VAT. At the end, the total legal, professional and administrators fees totalled well over £1.2m – money which would come out of the proceeds of the sale.

The report also concluded that CCFC Ltd's total liabilities stood at £69m.

It said Sisu's parent company of CCFC Holdings, Sky Blue Sports and Leisure, was owed £14m; Holdings £44m; ACL £636,381 (which deducted matchday costs paid to ACL over the previous year); while Arvo was owed £10.2m.

There was some debate over where player contracts and registrations sat, and it later emerged there had been errors made when registering players.

The club's owners contended that the Football League 'golden share' sat in Holdings – the club not in administration – as a result of players being registered in that firm. But the Football League and the administrator appeared to disagree and Mr Appleton insisted the 'rights, title or interest' of the company – including the golden share – was up for grabs.

That meant Sisu could face a challenge for ownership of the club, and they did.

A formal takeover bid was submitted to the administrator by Preston Haskell.

The US tycoon had been supported in his bid by suspended life president Joe Elliott and former vice-chairman Gary Hoffman. For the first time, exactly what was contained in that bid can be revealed after a copy of the offer document was sent to me as I compiled research for this book.

In relation to the purchase price, the offer letter read: 'The aggregate consideration for the purchase of the target business will be £7.5m payable one-time upfront. £750,000 from the above purchase price will be utilised to cover the administrators' fees.'

The offer also outlined a number of additional benefits. It pledged additional payments for the next five seasons, but only one qualifying payment per season.

They included £100,000 if the club was in the League One play-offs; £250,000 if the club was in the League One play-off final; and £1m if the club was promoted to Championship.

Over the next ten seasons, it promised one additional payment a season of £250,000 if the club reached the Championship play-offs; £500,000 if CCFC reached the Championship play-off final; and £5m if promoted to Premier League.

Furthermore, there would be payments of £2.5mif Premier League status was retained for each of the next two seasons and £5m for two consecutive seasons following after the initial one.

There were also payments promised for cup competitions over the next five seasons, including £250,000 for reaching Football League Trophy Final; £100,000 for reaching League Cup semi-final; £250,000 for reaching League Cup Final; £100,000 for reaching FA Cup quarter-final; £250,000 for reaching FA Cup semi-final and £500,000 for reaching FA Cup Final.

Over the next 15 years, it promised payments of £2mif the club qualified for the Europa League and £3m if they ever reached the Champions League. The offer was subject to certain conditions, including due diligence and being awarded the 'golden share' by the Football League.

Preston Haskell signed off the offer with a short statement, which read: 'I believe that my proposed offer is highly favourable and attractive to CCFC.

'I am enthusiastic about this opportunity and committed to dedicating substantial time and financial resources with a view to concluding a transaction as soon as possible.'

Asked just how committed to the cause Preston Haskell was, Joe Elliott replied: 'Preston wanted the lot, the club and the stadium. He offered almost £8m up front to the administrator for CCFC Ltd and a further option of £18.5m on achievement over the next ten years.

'That was based on how the club performed in the league and whether it reached cup semi-finals and so on.

'That was an indicative offer sent to the administrator in writing the day before the final offers had to go in. He had a substantial budget to buy the club and the Arena if he could.

'He showed us very substantial proof of funds, which we showed to the administrator. The proof of funds was also signed off by a well-known group of legal experts in Birmingham and London as being in order.

'He had also had discussions with the Higgs Charity about buying their share in ACL.

'That was, I thought, a reasonable offer to the administrator.'

Former vice-chairman Gary Hoffman also said he believed the Haskell bid was serious, although it was always at a disadvantage due to the debt CCFC Ltd owed to Sisu-owned companies.

He said: 'Preston Haskell made an offer to the administrator with proof of funds for £20m.

'Sisu always said publicly this guy hasn't got the money. He sent proof of funds for £20m from banks and lawyers and made an offer.

'It was much more than Sisu offered, but they had the debt to put on top.

'They were always going to win unless they were prepared to write off the debt.

'This football club is worth a lot less than £1. You have to fund it and there are no assets.

'When I said we will give you £1, that was a damn good offer – because it would have stopped their losses and someone else would have paid for that.

'The administrator seemed fine with the bid. But we always suspected that he didn't really need it.

'He was in a difficult position. I don't blame him in that respect.'

Somewhat unexpectedly, there was also an early bid submitted by Ricoh Arena operator ACL. This was arguably a controversial move as it could have paved the way for a firm jointly owned by taxpayers to run a hugely loss-making football club.

But Peter Knatchbull-Hugessen, ACL director and clerk of the Higgs Charity, said the bid was only ever meant to be a fall-back option to preserve CCFC and protect ACL's business if no other serious bids were entered.

He said: 'ACL had put in a bid, but it was obvious the reason we were putting in the bid was as a fall-back.

'It would have been very difficult for us to put in a bid that seriously challenged.

'But we were obviously very dissatisfied with the whole administration process.'

Another challenger emerged in the shape of North Warwickshire businessman Michael Byng, who insisted he represented a consortium of Chinese and Asian would-be investors.

However, his bid was never received by the administrator and Mr Byng initially indicated the offer must have got lost in cyberspace after being sent by e-mail.

He later clarified the situation in an interview with the *Coventry Telegraph* in which he said: 'The Chinese are looking to get involved with the Ricoh Arena and football club, but not in the middle of the argument.

'They were extremely dissatisfied with what was going on. The reason they withheld their bid was they didn't understand what was going on – they didn't understand ACL's motives for making an indicative bid.

'They had understood ACL wanted to sell the Ricoh Arena.'

Ultimately, it was Sisu-owned company Otium Entertainment which secured CCFC Ltd and the coveted golden share – a move which also removed any possibility of a legal challenge from Sisu.

The administrator said the offer was 'substantially more' than other bids received. The result was largely unsurprising unless the existing owners decided to walk away with firms under Sisu control being owed tens of millions between them.

It later emerged that part of the deal had involved converting £61m of debt into shares as well as a goodwill payment of £1. Total payments amounted to about £1.5m, according to Companies House documents, with £1 paid for business and intellectual property, £2 for Football League and FA shares, £466,742 for player contracts, £1 for equipment, £5,000 for the IT system, £1m for any debts, guarantees and security rights (including an impending business rates rebate), £1 for 'contingent rights', £1 for licences, £1 for the business records and £28,254 for property rights and assets owned.

After announcing the winning bid, Mr Appleton said: 'Following a stringent sale process, I can confirm a bid has now been accepted from Otium Entertainment Group Limited.

'This offer allows me to achieve the purpose of the administration and, following discussions with the Football League, I am hopeful a completion of the sale can be achieved as swiftly as possible.

'I realise and appreciate the end result of the sale process will not necessarily be welcomed by a large number of Coventry City fans.

'However, the bid from Otium Entertainment Group Limited was substantially more than any of the other three bids received and was the bid which gave the greatest return to the unsecured, non-connected creditors of CCFC Limited by a considerable margin.'

Speaking shortly after the result, Preston Haskell confirmed he would be walking away from attempts to purchase the club.

He said: 'Over the past few months, while working hard to acquire CCFC, I have developed a strong affinity with the fanbase of the club.

'Of course I am disappointed by this afternoon's decision but I am incredibly proud to have had the experience and unforeseen encouragement of a lot of dedicated supporters. I'm so appreciative of that.

'I personally met with Paul Appleton and think he and his colleagues, bound by the laws and rules of an official legal process, have been very professional throughout this difficult undertaking. His job wasn't easy but it was done according to the law, and appropriately managed.

'I would also like to publicly thank the 'good and great of Coventry', Joe Elliott and the steadfast Gary Hoffman, for their unwavering support and hard work. These two gentlemen truly bleed Sky Blue.

'Finally, I sincerely hope for the best at CCFC.'

Coventry City (Holdings) released a statement after the result, which read: 'We are pleased with the decision which helps to assure the future of the club.

'Our absolute focus now is to exit CCFC Ltd from the administration process so we can get back to running a football club and make the decisions we need to in time for next season.'

But this was not the end of the road. There was still the small matter of the Company Voluntary Agreement which would decide how much each creditor received from the debt recovery process.

But ACL and HMRC both voted against the CVA after a ten-minute meeting on 2 August, leading to fears the club would be hit with a new 15-point deduction ahead of the new League One campaign following precedents at Leeds United and Luton Town. But in the end, the Football League settled on a further ten-point deduction ahead of the new season.

Speaking after the imposition of the penalty Greg Clarke, Football League chairman, said: 'Once again, it is a source of immense frustration to everyone involved that the two parties in this dispute have failed to reach any agreement. The board is dismayed at the level of intransigence being shown.

'Nonetheless, the league will continue with its efforts to get the two parties to enter into meaningful negotiations.

'The board's decision means that these attempts can now be conducted against a backdrop of Coventry City as a continuing member of the Football League, rather than it having to bring an end to the club's 94 years in league football.'

If ACL had agreed to the CVA, they would have seen a £590,000 return on the Sky Blues £1m-plus rent debt. Instead, they would later recoup £470,000 after a further year of wrangling.

The stadium firm said it rejected the deal because it wanted the administrator to include guarantees in the CVA, including those which would have ensured CCFC continued to play at the Ricoh Arena.

A statement from ACL read: 'This decision was based on ACL's twin aims: first, to keep Coventry City Football Club playing in Coventry; and second, to ensure that Coventry City Football Club is financially viable for the next few years and beyond.

'This last point is especially important given that CCFC has been the subject of a 'catastrophic insolvency' in the hands of its previous owners.

'The CVA proposals put forward by Mr Appleton simply do not address these obvious concerns. And these concerns are not only the concerns of ACL – they are the concerns of all Sky Blues' supporters and should be the central concerns of both the Football League and the Football Association.

'Mr Appleton has the ability to put forward new proposals, and we would welcome these as soon as possible.'

But Paul Appleton said what ACL was asking was not within his power.

He said: 'Put simply, we do not understand the comments being made by ACL with regard to the ability to put forward new proposals. As I said , the proposals ACL required simply did not comply with the law.

'They were offered the chance to submit modifications which did comply with the law, yet for reasons best known to themselves, they chose not to do so.'

Following the meeting, Coventry City Football Club issued a statement expressing 'great regret' that ACL had rejected the agreement and highlighting that the Alan Higgs Centre Trust had voted in favour of it.

An important distinction here is that the Alan Higgs Centre Trust is a different organisation from the Higgs Charity – which is a 50 per cent shareholder in ACL. The Alan Higgs Centre Trust was responsible solely for the Alan Higgs Centre, in Allard Way, and was a creditor in relation to debts owed as a result of the academy using the facilities.

The Higgs Charity had no direct vote or interest in relation to the CVA, although it was a 50 per cent shareholder in ACL.

To confuse matters further, Peter Knatchbull-Hugessen had two votes – one as a board member of ACL and one as a board member of the Alan Higgs Centre Trust (not the Higgs Charity).

While representing the Alan Higgs Centre Trust (which, remember, is not the Higgs Charity and was simply responsible for CCFC's academy base), he voted to accept the CVA.

When representing ACL, he voted to reject the deal.

I asked him to explain his reasons for this seemingly odd voting pattern and he told me: 'The Alan Higgs Centre Trust, as a separate entity and with separate directors, voted with Sisu.

'That was because, in terms of continuing business, we thought it was better for the Centre Trust to get the CVA because that would see the academy continue at the Higgs Centre.

'The directors who decided on that were Joe Elliott, John Mutton and me.

'But then you have to change your hat as you have different responsibilities. ACL was against the CVA because we would have lost vast amounts of money.

'That's just directors acting as directors. It's not inconsistent, it's just people realising their responsibilities and acting properly and legally.'

Chapter Nine

Highfield Road II

I N May 2013, Coventry City Football Club's chief executive Tim Fisher made an announcement which would shock and divide Sky Blues fans.

He said that Coventry City had played their last game in the city which gave them their name and that plans were being progressed for a new stadium in the 'Coventry area'.

Talks over a deal to continue at the Ricoh Arena had failed after Sisu boss Joy Seppala had pulled the plug on a new rental deal provisionally agreed in January with the Sky Blues. Ms Seppala was adamant that any deal for the club to remain at the Ricoh Arena had to involve some form of stadium ownership.

Few bought into the vision at the time, with many questioning how a club in such a dire financial situation could possibly afford to build a new ground. Others insisted it was nothing more than a negotiating tactic as Sisu sought to agree a better deal at the Ricoh Arena.

But Mr Fisher remained typically bullish, and even insisted the process of acquiring land had already begun with a view to having the stadium completed during 2016.

Speaking during an interview with the *Coventry Telegraph* at the time, he said: 'People have to understand we do not posture, we do not threaten, because that is not how you do business. You only do business in good faith. Always.

'We have started the process of procuring land so that we can shift the new stadium build forward at a pace. The stadium will be in the Coventry area in accordance with Football League rules.

'We have left the Ricoh Arena. We were told categorically by ACL and by the council that there was no commercial deal to be done and, in actual fact, they would only ever work with the administrator.

'We were very, very clear in our minds as to exactly what was intended. Given the position, we have had to make contingency plans to fulfil our fixtures on an interim basis while we deliver the long-term vision.

'That long-term vision has us playing in the Coventry area in a new stadium that will be designed and delivered in three years.

'All this will be in full consultation with the fans – starting with the upcoming forums.

'In consideration of financial fair play, then we will own all the revenue streams that come from matchday and non-matchday activities, and therefore we will have every chance of becoming a solid, vibrant club.'

ACL, of course, disputed that there was 'no deal to be done' and insisted the doors to the Ricoh Arena remained open.

The firm's lawyer, James Powell, also raised questions about how a club in Coventry's situation could afford to build a new ground.

Speaking to BBC Coventry and Warwickshire, he said: 'I was surprised and taken aback. My personal impression was that this was an announcement made on the hoof.

'There's not been any suggestion of another stadium in and around Coventry in anything Mr Fisher or the club have been saying over the last few months.

'The Football League are looking for a whole host of things. A ground in the vicinity of Coventry is one of those things, but a club with financial stability is far more important.

'Mr Fisher is a director, or the director, of a company that, according to the administrator's report, is £70m in debt and was described as a "catastrophic insolvency" by the administrator's own barrister.

'You'd be asking the question "Mr Fisher, where are you getting the money from, given that you've managed to lose £70m over the last few years?"'

But Tim Fisher continued to provide details of the plans and said the club had even hired specialist advisers to help complete the project.

He told the *Coventry Telegraph*: 'We retained specialists some months ago to advise us on where to build a new stadium for the club in the immediate Coventry area. We are not leaving Coventry in the long term.'

Further details began to leak to the press, including a clever piece of PR which involved labelling the new stadium project 'Highfield Two'.

The reference was a nod back to Coventry City's home of 106 years and a clear attempt to pull at the supporters' heart strings and foster an emotional connection with the new stadium proposals.

It was a shrewd move. Many fans were unhappy with the club leaving its historic former 23,000-capacity Highfield Road stadium in Hillfields, near the city centre, for the larger 32,000-capacity Ricoh Arena on the city's outskirts, which was more difficult to get to.

But there were still more questions than answers. Where would it be? How big would it be? How much would it cost? Do you need to have seen Highfield Road One to enjoy the sequel?

Details leaked to the *Coventry Telegraph* by club officials in the early weeks after the announcement disclosed that the new stadium would be in a secret location just outside the city boundary, but that it would also be closer to the city centre than the Ricoh Arena.

Initial plans were said to be based on Rotherham United's 12,000-seater New York Stadium, which took four years to build.

Club directors claimed they were impressed with the South Yorkshire club's ground as it was completed at a cost of just £20m.

It was also viewed as a suitable model to follow as it was a 'modular' project – meaning more capacity could be added if the club achieved promotion and increased attendances.

Club officials also told the *Coventry Telegraph* that they had kept the Football League fully informed about the plan.

There would, of course, be hoops to jump through. The Football League usually only allowed clubs to play home fixtures outside their home town or city if any temporary ground-share arrangement was within a 30-mile radius - and the club has a clear business plan to return to their home city within a designated period.

Rotherham United were given four years, but Coventry City were claiming their plans could be completed within three.

The location of this new stadium would become a topic of much focus over the coming months and years.

Initially, the club said five sites just outside Coventry's administrative boundary had been identified by property agents employed by Sisu and CCFC Holdings Ltd, headed by Tim Fisher.

But they insisted – even at this very early stage – that one site had already become the preferred option and a bid put in to compete with other offers.

Club officials were already indicating that sites outside the Coventry boundary were being explored due to the bad blood between the owners and Coventry City Council.

This stance seemed odd from the outset as Coventry City Council's planning committee, as with any other council's, is strictly legally obliged to vote based on 'material planning considerations', not on prejudices or party political lines. In other words, the council could not turn down a planning application because councillors didn't like the person applying – and if they did the council could potentially face severe legal repercussions and their decision could be overridden.

Another hurdle the club would face is that any site chosen would likely be green belt land. But they pointed to planning guidelines issued relatively recently which instructs council planning committees to make decisions with a 'presumption in favour of sustainable development.' Sports grounds were also given special treatment in the new planning regulations.

Some fans questioned the need for a new stadium while the Ricoh Arena, built for the football club less than a decade ago, would be sitting empty.

But Tim Fisher suggested the move to the Ricoh Arena was a mistake from the beginning.

In June, he told a fans' forum: 'The accounts have been a mess, an absolute mess.

'You can trace mistakes back to 1995 – basically it was slovenly long before Sisu came on the scene.

'The problems started the day they left Highfield Road, so we need to get our own stadium so that all revenues generated will go to the football team.'

He later told fans, in a tongue-in-cheek fashion: 'They should put a statue of Joy Seppala outside the ground for the £45m she has put into the club.'

He later pointed to the conduct of ACL during the administration process as another reason why the club could not stay at the Ricoh Arena.

Speaking shortly after the Creditors Voluntary Agreement had been rejected by ACL, he said: 'We can now get on and put our future plans into action, which means building and owning our own stadium in the Coventry area.

'It has been a very difficult time but Coventry City Football Club moves forward.

'Surely the events of the last few days and the abuse of the administration process highlight that the club had been left with very little room for manoeuvre.

'Indeed, I am sure that all the fans are aware that the very reason ACL stated for filing for administration in the first place was to avoid liquidation and a points deduction this season.

'Liquidation is exactly what they pushed for and succeeded in getting today.'

The hunt for the new stadium was on, but trying to uncover details about it and where it would be was not easy. In fact, it felt at times as if it would have been easier to prove the existence of unicorns. The new stadium, of course, was never built. Some doubt it ever really existed other than in the minds of certain club/Sisu officials.

Having investigated this matter more thoroughly than any other media outlet, I have to say there has never been any solid proof for its existence.

I would accept that there may have been a desire to build a new ground at a very early stage. But it appears to me that at some point this became little more than a negotiating tool and was simply posturing by club officials and Sisu.

It is impossible to definitively prove that something doesn't exist. All you can do is provide as much evidence as possible and allow people to make informed decisions – and so that's what I dedicated my investigative journalism skills to after arriving at the Coventry Telegraph in July 2013.

Obviously we know the stadium was never built.

But let's look at some of the developments and rumours which have emerged to date in relation to the new stadium project.

In May 2013, Coventry City had appointed property agents CBRE, who said a deal for stadium land was likely to be 'weeks away'. The firm said it had been instructed to secure a deal to pave the way for firm stadium proposals to go to the Football League the following month.

A CBRE spokesman told the *Coventry Telegraph*: 'CBRE is advising Sisu, owner of Coventry City Football Club, on the club's proposed relocation.

'The firm has been working on finding a site for a new stadium within the Coventry area and is close to agreeing a land deal.

'This will secure the future of the club going forward, providing first-class new facilities for the team, fans and the local community. Proposals will go before the Football League in June.'

Mr Fisher said he expected a purchase to be completed within 'three to four weeks' but still refused to name the site, which he insisted had moved to a second round of bidding. He also declined to identify back-up sites, saying they must remain confidential for commercial reasons.

In July 2013, it was reported that the football club had signed a provisional agreement to purchase land in Brandon, although no official confirmation or evidence of this deal has ever emerged. The land in question was the area occupied by Coventry Stadium – the home of the Coventry Bees speedway team. Quite what any deal would have meant for the speedway team had it been completed was never made clear.

However, no deal was ever completed by the football club and the land was eventually sold off with a view to building housing on the site – although the battle to save the home of Coventry Bees continues to this day.

Apparent problems with the Brandon deal appeared to prompt a slight shift in position from club officials. Having previously said the club would never play at the Ricoh Arena again, Mr Fisher now said a return might be possible – if ownership was on the table. There was also a subtle change in the timeline for the new stadium construction up from three years to 'three to five years'.

In August 2013, shortly after the club had begun to play 'home matches' at Sixfields (which we will cover in the coming chapters), he told the *Coventry Telegraph*: 'The club was expecting the council to consider whether it wished to renew discussions on the basis on a transaction, but no response has been received.

'The club simply needs all the revenue which comes from owning its own stadium.'

In response to scepticism from fans over the project, he added: 'If we say we're going to build a stadium, then we will. We have provided clear evidence to the league on our ability to deliver on those plans. It's not, and never will be, our intention to mislead, filibuster or posture.

'Overall, our primary objective was to fulfil our fixtures with a ground-share. People questioned whether we would proceed. We've done that.

'Our second objective is to develop a site to capture all the revenues from stadium.'

As the end of 2013 approached, other sites apparently considered by the football club appeared to be ruled out by owners – including land owned by Coventry University and Warwick University.

The owners of the former Peugeot factory site in Ryton also said no approach had been made, as did landowners at Ansty Park.

But CBRE insisted plans were still being progressed.

In a statement released in September 2013, it said: 'We are continuing to work closely with the club to find a suitable location, with four potential sites currently being considered, one of which we have agreed terms on, and this continues to progress well.

'Due diligence on the site is likely to take a further four weeks.

'As previously confirmed, we have short-listed a handful of sites, all of which are within six miles of Coventry city centre.

'Remaining close to the club's fanbase is one of the key drivers in the site selection process. Vectos, appointed transport consultants on the project, are looking at each of the sites to ensure they will be easily accessible to the fans.

'Likewise, we are working closely with the other advisers on the project, including planners [Turleys] and architects [AFLS+P], to ensure its ultimate deliverability.

'Otium has invested significant financial resources in the project to date and continue to do so to ensure expedient completion of the stadium within the Coventry area.

'Those sites which we are currently in discussions on are commercially sensitive and it would not be appropriate to release this information at the current time.

'CBRE is providing regular updates to the Football League as part of the process.'

Sisu chief executive Joy Seppala even waded in to add weight to the new stadium plans. Later that month, she took part in an interview with the *Coventry Telegraph*.

She said: 'Plan A is building a new stadium. There is something very exciting about building something that is a new beginning. It feels like the club is at a new beginning.

'The business side is operationally in a good place. Tim Fisher's done a good job. The football side is going well.

'What's exciting is being involved in the beginning to the end of building something like that, from purchasing land to planning permission to the designs for the stadium. Building it is exciting, different and new.

'Things have moved on since the Ricoh. The ability to expand [as the club grows] is exciting. We can start smaller and then build around it, whether or not it's a multi-purpose sports stadium.

'We could have various sporting events there from a business model perspective and develop around it, whether it's retail, restaurants or homes. There is a lot of flexibility in how we develop it. It's something we would relish. It's a dream.'

She added: 'Most councils would love the idea of having a football club, given the economic impact it has.

'The new stadium will be close to Coventry but not in the jurisdiction of Coventry City Council. We met the Football

League in January and discussed where it should be and what it should be.

'Instinctively, it would not cross my mind to have it within Coventry City Council's boundary given the history, histrionics and the issue of freehold ownership.

'I am not concerned about the funding of a stadium. I'm reasonably comfortable that won't be an issue.

'I have got people who are more than happy to fund that. I'm having discussions all the time with investors.'

But, with an apparent lack of public progress over the new stadium, fans continued to question whether the new stadium plans were an idea based in reality.

In December, as attendances suffered massively following the the club's move to play 'home' games in Northampton, the owners upped the ante with a massive publicity drive for the new stadium.

Flashy images were unveiled by architects AFLS+P and the club also formed the CCFC Stadium Forum with respected lawyer Sandra Garlick at its helm. The purpose of the group was to allow supporters to have input over what should be included in the new stadium.

In a statement issued at the time of her appointment, Sandra Garlick said: 'The purpose of the Stadium Forum is to provide a voice for fans when it comes to the creation of the new ground.

'Having met with members of the Coventry City Football Club board and the owner, I have seen both their enthusiasm and determination to create a new stadium that brings a range of commercial benefits to the club. The board and the owner want the fans to be at the heart of the whole process.

'The benefits to owning a new stadium are not just financial but will also allow the club to offer an even greater community provision to supporters – something which is very close to my heart as a trustee of Sky Blues in the Community. That can mean anything from health and education to social enterprise.

'As a supporter, it has been very difficult to see the club playing outside the region and the new stadium plans are vital in getting Coventry City back in the Coventry area.

'I am also here in a very neutral capacity and have experience in listening to different views and condensing them down into workable recommendations.

'I very much look forward to working with fellow supporters on this project for the lasting benefit of the club, its fans and the community.'

The CCFC Stadium Forum held its first meeting in January 2014, and I attended. But, in truth, the whole thing seemed utterly bizarre. No stadium site had been identified but a group was set up to debate and decide things such as the colour of carpets and curtains at the new ground.

The group eventually became a subject of ridicule among many supporters and was ultimately shut down in 2015.

Accompanying the images, and new stadium talking shop, was a lengthy Q&A about exactly what the new stadium project entailed. It was posted on the CCFC official website and addressed questions such as 'What is the inspiration behind the outer design?' and 'What will the capacity of the stadium be?'

The Q&A revealed that the project would ideally include first team and academy training facilities on one site and that it would likely be in excess of 50-acres.

Tim Fisher was quoted as saying: 'The size of the plot is key given that the stadium build is only phase one of the whole project. For phase two, we will introduce the academy and first-team training facilities. We have a unique opportunity to consolidate all our physical resources on one site.

'The stadium and academy site will also be a community hub and will promote sport, health, education, employment and training, social enterprise and social inclusion for all.'

He added: 'The design will be modular in the sense that the stadium capacity will grow as the club becomes more successful. Initially, we are proposing a capacity of 12-13,000.

The next stage of the club's development will see the capacity grow to 15-17,000. We believe that, ultimately, the stadium capacity will target some 21–23,000.

'The first-draft stadium brief also includes ten 12-seat hospitality boxes, one 24-seat hospitality box, a 100-seat silver service restaurant and a 430-seat function room.'

The comments on relocating the academy to any new site would eventually come back to haunt the club. They were made at a sensitive time, with club and Higgs Centre bosses having agreed the academy could return to the venue just ten days earlier. That agreement followed months of wrangling over maintenance costs following CCFC Ltd entering administration.

At the time of writing, the academy's future was in serious doubt with the club's agreement to remain at the Higgs Centre due to expire in June 2017. Higgs Centre bosses said they had to explore other uses for the site as a direct result of CCFC's statements about relocating the academy. Whether the academy can continue at the Higgs Centre, or another site, in its current level remained to be seen.

In December 2013, Coventry City's chief executive Tim Fisher and the club's development director were continuing to talk up the new stadium vision.

Tim Fisher said: 'We are very pleased and excited to be able to share these initial images with supporters as, ultimately, we want this to be a home the fans can be proud of.

'A great deal of time, effort and investment has gone into bringing the plans to this stage and it has been a real team effort to develop the technical aspects of the stadium.

'We've come a long, long way in a very short space of time as we only reconstituted the club in August and are now announcing our plans for the new stadium.

'I understand that the key question on everybody's lips is, "where is it going to be?" We are working very hard with CBRE to purchase our preferred site and we will, of course, keep supporters informed when that happens.

'At that stage, we can then start to plot a timeline of applying for permission, time it takes to build and when we could open.

'There is still a huge amount of effort required and I would urge supporters to make full use of the stadium forum that has been set up so their views can help to shape how we make this a home for the club and its fans.'

Steve Waggott added: 'There are several ingredients for creating a sustainable and successful club and owning your own ground is one of the main ingredients.

'A football club needs to squeeze every penny it possibly can out of its stadium, both on match days and non-match days, in order to be able to invest on the pitch. Owning our own stadium, as well as investing in our academy and youth development, are the key to the long-term future of the club.'

As we entered 2014, and with so much buzz being created about the new stadium but little sign of obvious progress, I took it upon myself to uncover as much information as possible about where this new stadium would be.

With public authorities, consultants, the Football League and the club all unwilling, or unable, to reveal which sites were being considered for development, this was easier said than done.

So I turned to the trusty Freedom of Information (FOI) Act. For those who aren't *au fait* with the finer details of geeky investigative journalism techniques, this wonderful piece of legislation allows members of the public to obtain information held by public authorities – in this case councils and government agencies.

It's important to clarify exactly what these authorities can and cannot do in relation to FOI requests. They can refuse to provide certain documents if they would breach commercial confidentiality or they can heavily redact information provided. They cannot, however, lie about whether or not they hold certain information.

To uncover whether, at the very least, discussions about developing a large sporting stadia had been held with relevant parties, I submitted a bunch of Freedom of Information requests. These were sent to organisations which, according to an independent planning expert, would routinely be consulted ahead of any land deal for a project of this size.

They included nine local authorities – Coventry, Solihull, Hinckley and Bosworth, North Warwickshire, Warwick, Warwickshire, Nuneaton and Bedworth, Daventry and Stratford councils.

Also contacted were the Department For Transport/ The Highways Agency, The Environment Agency and The Department for Culture Media and Sport.

The office of the Secretary of State for Communities and Local Government and the police forces in Warwickshire, Leicester, Northampton and the West Midlands were also contacted, along with the University of Warwick and Coventry University.

All bar Nuneaton and Bedworth Borough Council denied having contact with any organisation about the development of a large sporting stadium within the previous 18 months.

Club officials sought to dismiss the findings on the basis that public bodies would not disclose commercially confidential information – but this was incorrect.

As previously covered, the fact that denials were issued was key as public bodies cannot deliberately mislead in their responses to FOI requests. Had they declined to answer on the basis of commercial confidentiality, that would have been a different matter. But they didn't. They categorically said there had been no contact in the 18 months up to January 2014.

Those findings were also backed up by similar subsequent FOI requests from the Sky Blue Trust supporters group.

Nuneaton and Bedworth did confirm contact but insisted that amounted to a single speculative enquiry.

Nuneaton council leader Dennis Harvey said: 'I can confirm that an enquiry has been made by a developer to council officers. However, this was of a very speculative nature and at an early stage.

'Since that initial exploratory contact, we have received no further approach and we are therefore not considering any proposal for any particular location.'

Eleanor Deeley, of the club's property consultants CBRE, scrambled to provide me with an explanation for the findings.

She told me: 'The team is only contacting organisations which we feel – based on expert advice – to be relevant at this early stage in the whole development process.

'The planning consultant is correct that if we were preparing a planning application right now, we would have contacted many of those on the list provided.

'However, as we have outlined previously, we are not at the stage of submitting a planning application. We are currently purchasing the land.

'This is why we are working with professional planning consultants – they assess the potential for planning on a site such as this.

'We said at the forums we are working towards applications on two sites. Everything is geared to that but we will not be at the stage of submitting the applications until the land is purchased.'

She added: 'Revealing the preferred location for a new stadium would not be in the best interests of the club or in the best interests of delivering a new stadium.

'The club are committed to delivering a new stadium and have, therefore, taken the advice of their consultants that until all legal agreements have completed they will not be releasing the location of the preferred site.

'Our objective is to deliver a stadium as swiftly as possible. However, we have to work within the confines of the planning system.

'A planning application will take around six months to prepare as it is likely to require an Environmental Impact Assessment.

'There are then statutory timescales for the planning process and also the possibility that the application may have to go to appeal or may be called in. But the objective is to get the club back in the Coventry area as soon as possible.'

The results of the *Coventry Telegraph* investigation and enquiries from supporters' group the Sky Blue Trust were clearly causing headaches for club officials, who continued to peddle the new stadium line.

I was soon contacted by club board member Mark Labovitch, who was never one to miss an opportunity to try to spin a story in a certain direction.

Our conversation resulted in one of his most famous quotes of the entire saga.

He told me: 'We are about three weeks away from being able to name the final site. We are down to two sites and hopefully, within a month, two will be down to one.

'I don't like the position of no comment, but the commercial and political sensitivity around land negotiations is such that we cannot talk about individual sites yet.'

Three weeks later, we were no closer to finding out the location of the new stadium. I also understand Mr Labovitch subsequently tried to suggest he had been 'misquoted' during that particular interview. I can tell you two things in relation to that claim: he never once complained directly to me that he had been misquoted in that interview, and he wasn't misquoted in that interview.

I repeated the round of FOIs 12 months after Mr Labovitch's 'three weeks' timescale in January 2015 – and this time every single organisation contacted said they had not had any contact over the potential development of a large sports stadium.

Later that month, Tim Fisher, who had now moved to the role of club chairman, told the CCFC Stadium Forum that three sites had been ruled out for a new stadium.

According to extracts from the minutes of the meeting, Mr Fisher said the football club had looked at, and ruled out, three sites which fall in Rugby Borough Council's boundary – Prologis Park, in Ryton, as well as another site at Ansty Park and the existing home of Coventry Speedway, in Brandon.

Mr Fisher also claimed club representatives had been in discussions with the council about the potential of these three sites as the base for a new Sky Blues stadium.

But, oddly, Rugby Borough Council said just weeks before this meeting: 'Rugby Borough Council has not engaged in any formal conversations with any individual/organisation about any proposed new large sporting stadia with spectator seating within the council boundary area over the past 12 months.'

Tim Fisher's claims also directly contradicted evidence uncovered through the *Coventry Telegraph's* stadium investigation and the responses received under the Freedom of Information Act.

In March 2015, I pressed Mr Fisher on how any new stadium arrangement would be financed, bearing in mind the club's financial difficulties. Surprisingly, he told me that the club would have to pay rent at any new stadium.

Tim Fisher said any new stadium build would likely take place under a structure known as a 'propco-opco' arrangement.

In simple terms, that would involve setting up a property company to raise funds and build the stadium, while a separate stadium operating company – the football club in this instance – would operate the venue and benefit from all the revenues generated at the stadium.

However, there would also be a commitment from the operating company to enter into a rental agreement with the property company to allow the club to receive all stadium revenues, both matchday and non-matchday.

That would allow any debts accrued by the property company – such as those acquired in the construction of the stadium – to be kept separate from the operating company.

Tim Fisher said: 'The capital cost would be met by a separate company, a property company. That's the norm throughout football whenever projects like this are undertaken.

'The absolutely crucial thing here is that the football club would benefit from all match day and non-match day revenues generated at the stadium.

'Under the rules that now govern football – either financial fair play or salary cost management protocol – that allows us to get the best possible team on the pitch.'

In April 2015, I revealed that high-level talks between Rugby Borough Council and Coventry City FC had taken place in March 2015. But redacted minutes obtained from the meeting following an FOI request did little to convince supporters the new stadium was a reality.

One startling admission was that no formal plans had been drawn up for the new stadium despite the plans first being announced almost exactly two years previously – with the aim of them being delivered within three years.

The new stadium discussion is one which is still very much rumbling on at the time of writing. The opinion that it is little more than a negotiating tool as the football club aims to secure its long-term future at the Ricoh Arena seems to be the view widely taken. And you can't blame the club for that in some ways. Why wouldn't they adopt a stance which gives them a commercial advantage in negotiations?

During 2016, we have seen the suggestion that the club could seek to ground-share with Coventry Rugby Club at a redeveloped Butts Park Arena.

The *Coventry Telegraph* revealed that formal discussions had taken place between rugby club bosses and football club officials in May 2016. It was another clever PR move by the football club and its owners as the idea of a city centre ground is something which would obviously appeal to many Coventry City supporters – as would a closer relationship with Coventry Rugby Club.

But (at the time of writing) any possible ground-share deal at the Butts Park Arena had failed to get out of the starting blocks and land leaseholder Chris Millerchip (a former Coventry RFC player), had poured cold water on the plans.

During investigations for this book, I learned that Chris Millerchip is a friend of Sisu co-founder Dermot Coleman. The two played rugby together during their time at Oxford University and Dermot Coleman arranged a meeting between Sisu chief Joy Seppala and Chris Millerchip.

I'm told those discussions were initially very positive, but Chris Millerchip had insisted that peace talks be held between Sisu, Coventry City Council and other involved parties before any progress could be made on plans for any new stadium at The Butts. Chris Millerchip, who estimates he has invested almost half a million pounds in Coventry RFC, also wanted to ensure the long-term future of the rugby club. The previous fall-out around CCFC and the Ricoh Arena had made the former Henry VIII schoolboy anxious.

I understand Coventry Olympian and former 5,000-metre world record holder David Moorcroft and Coventry Cathedral's Rev John Witcombe agreed to act as mediators between Sisu, the council and other organisations.

But days before it was due to take place, a scheduled meeting between Joy Seppala and Mr Moorcroft was cancelled and never rearranged.

Where any possible new stadium for the Sky Blues might be is as much of a mystery at time of writing as it has ever been.

Of course, the idea that Coventry City FC has to build its own stadium might gain more traction if those at the top of CCFC and Sisu made sure they were on the same page before issuing public statements on the subject.

In February, Joy Seppala told Coventry City FC supporters the club must own its own stadium in order to be viable as a club in the long term.

She made the comments during a Q&A session with the Supporters Consultative Group (SCG), when she is recorded as saying 'a new stadium is essential for the viability of the club in the long run' in minutes published on the CCFC website.

But a few days later Chris Anderson, managing director of CCFC, told me: 'I think there can be a solution that doesn't involve us owning the stadium.'

He added: 'Manchester City don't own their own stadium, Swansea City share with a rugby club. Every situation is idiosyncratic.'

Chapter 10
Sent from Coventry

O N 22 March 2013, Coventry City FC pulled all of their staff out of the Ricoh Arena offices as striking images emerged of removal vans clearing out the contents of the stadium-based club shop.

For many, it was the first real sign that this dispute could actually result in the club leaving the Ricoh Arena.

Just 24 hours earlier, the club had entered administration and it was still not clear if they would be able to finish the season.

A statement released by Coventry City at the time read: 'The club has taken the decision to protect its staff by moving them from the stadium.

'Ideally, we would like to keep playing our home matches at the Ricoh if the stadium owners, Arena Coventry Ltd [ACL], will offer reasonable commercial terms.

'All we've ever asked for is an affordable rent with access to matchday revenues, like any other club. We hope these will be offered to us by ACL.

'We noted that the owners of the stadium, ACL, told the court they would be prepared to assist their proposed administrator "with a partial (or possibly full) deferral" of the stadium rent and licence fee during the administration process.

'Following Thursday's decision to place Coventry City Football Club Limited into administration, ACL told the appointed administrators they would require the full rent and licence fee on the stadium to be paid.

'To reach an agreement with ACL to allow the club to move back and fulfil its fixtures at the Ricoh Arena, we would hope and expect ACL would extend the same terms to the club.'

ACL responded swiftly with a short statement of their own, which read: 'The board wishes also to reiterate that there is no truth whatsoever in suggestions reported by some media that ACL will prevent CCFC from playing at the Ricoh Arena.

'The whole point of the course of legal action that the board has taken is to ensure that a successful and sustainable Sky Blues team is able to play at the Ricoh Arena for many years to come.'

Coventry City's chief executive Tim Fisher also reiterated the club's desire to see out the season at the Ricoh Arena.

He said: 'We appreciate that our supporters have been through a great deal of upset and uncertainty, and there is a responsibility on all parties to ensure that the question of where we play our remaining three home games is resolved as soon as possible. Allowing supporters to watch the Sky Blues at the Ricoh for three games would be a sensible step forward. We have contacted ACL and hope to have some clarity in the next 24 hours.'

An agreement for the club to see out its final three games of the season was agreed shortly afterwards.

Despite the events of the past 18 months, there can surely have been few inside the Ricoh Arena for that final game of the season against Leyton Orient who truly believed the Sky Blues would not be back at the Ricoh Arena for 2013/14.

The home campaign was seen out with an underwhelming 1-0 defeat and Sky Blues supporters were set for the longest summer break in their club's history.

It would be another 503 days – one year, four months and 16 days – before Coventry City played in their home city again.

Days after the end of the 2012/13 season, the club officially confirmed it would not play at the Ricoh Arena during the next season. The club blamed ACL and said they were 'locked out of the Ricoh', but stadium bosses insisted the club was welcome to stay, saying the doors 'remain wide open'.

Tim Fisher told the *Coventry Telegraph*: 'The fact is that we are being locked out of the Ricoh Arena. We have been told that there is no further room for negotiation and an offer that we made to get back round the negotiating table has been rejected.

'It is with great regret that we now have no alternative but to consider other arrangements for next season and we would be failing the club, its supporters and its staff if we did not start making such plans now.

'The club is keeping the relevant football authorities fully informed of developments, and we will keep everyone informed when there is specific further news.'

But James Powell, the lawyer representing ACL, quickly retaliated: 'We are absolutely flabbergasted by Tim Fisher's statement.

'Mr Fisher is the sole director of Coventry City Football Club Limited, a company that is now in administration as a result of a "catastrophic insolvency" in the words of the barrister acting for the administrator.

'To compound this issue, Mr Fisher is now suggesting that Coventry City Football Club should play their games outside Coventry. We have to question on this basis alone whether he is acting in the best interests of the football club.

'So that there can be no doubt in the minds of Sky Blues supporters, ACL have not locked the football club out of the Ricoh Arena. ACL have consistently acted to try to save the football club and to ensure that the football club continues to play at the Ricoh Arena. Indeed, ACL has already committed a significant level of funding to ensure that the pitch is improved for next season, after the club ceased to commit investment in the pitch towards the end of last season.

'Sky Blues supporters should be told on whose behalf Mr Fisher is making these statements.

'The football club, as acknowledged by The Football League in imposing a ten-point deduction, is in administration. Only the administrator should be making statements on behalf of the club at this time.'

He added: 'So that there can be no doubt whatsoever among Sky Blues fans, ACL would be delighted for Coventry City Football Club to play at the Ricoh Arena next season. Nobody connected to the football club has yet approached ACL in this regard.

'We simply cannot comprehend Mr Fisher's statement that he has supposedly been told that there is no room for negotiation or that negotiations have been rejected. If Mr Fisher has been told that, it was certainly not by anyone connected with ACL.

'Far from being locked, the Arena doors remain wide open, and ACL remains resolutely committed to preserving Coventry City as a successful league club, and playing its games at the Ricoh Arena in Coventry, where it belongs.'

A Football League spokesman confirmed: 'We have had, and are continuing to have, discussions with the club. At this stage, there has been no formal application lodged requesting a move to a specific location.'

Things were clearly getting nasty. As well as the public grandstanding, Sisu had also launched an application for a judicial review into the £14.4m Coventry City Council loan to ACL covered in the previous chapters.

But the petty side of the Ricoh Arena row had also started to emerge. Higgs Charity clerk and ACL director Peter Knatchbull-Hugessen had apparently been caught tying 'Sisu Out' balloons to Mr Fisher's car after a game at Crawley.

The football club chief executive apparently responded by threatening Arena Coventry Limited director Peter

Knatchbull-Hugessen with his 11-stone English Mastiff, called Hector.

One source told the *Coventry Telegraph* that Mr Fisher said the dog would next time 'eat' Mr Knatchbull-Hugessen, who was with fellow ACL director Paul Harris at the time.

I have to interject at this point. Having met Hector during a meeting in Tim Fisher's office at Ryton, I think this accusation is unfair. Despite his obviously large frame, Hector came across as a gentle soul who would not purposely inflict harm on anyone. I think any suggestion he would 'eat' a person is an unfair stain on his character.

Speaking about the incident shortly afterwards, Mr Knatchbull-Hugessen said. 'I'm pleading the fifth [amendment].

He added: 'It isn't a question of being anti-Sisu. Let's have some proper business discussion.'

When the incident was again brought up during the Higgs Charity High Court Battle with Sisu in 2014, he said: 'I have been specific that I am not and have not been orchestrating a "Sisu Out" campaign.

'I had no knowledge of it and no part of it and this is what I mean by wild accusations.'

He added: 'I can say on oath I have never tied a balloon to Mr Fisher's car. I placed a half-deflated balloon under his windscreen wiper.'

Another person who apparently had little love for Sisu was former defence secretary and MP Bob Ainsworth who represented the Coventry North East constituency where the Ricoh Arena was situated.

Over the next few months, he would go on to launch a series of high-profile attacks on the owners of the football club, condemning their actions in relation to the Ricoh Arena.

Speaking during an address to Parliament in March 2013, he said: 'Many of us accept the need for a realistic approach to the lease and management issues if the stadium is to reach its full potential and changes would get support for the right partner at the right time.

'But Sisu are not entitled to bully their way to control over an asset they never provided. They must prove they are not simply a predator with greed running through their DNA before they could expect such treatment.

'The club owners have been on rent strike. They say they are fighting for a more realistic settlement for a League One club, while Arena Coventry Limited, jointly owned by the city council and the Alan Higgs Charity, believe the agenda has been to destabilise the Arena Company and thereby gain control at a fire sale price. A much lowered rent has been offered but the dispute goes on.'

But, during a candid interview for this book, Mr Ainsworth said he had not always opposed Sisu's ownership and had initially tried to support them.

He said: 'The first person to contact me from the club was John Clarke [CCFC board member]. I think he contacted me because he had heard my view was that the Ricoh Arena should be sold.

'We met over coffee. I thought at one point he was going to offer me a place on the board or something, but he soon realised that I wasn't even a Sky Blues fan.

'I was then invited to the directors' dining room for lunch and a game by Rajay Naik who is a member of the Labour Party [and was a CCFC advisory board member].

'Onye Igwe was in charge then, but he never even spoke to me. It appeared to me set up so Mark Labovitch [then non-executive director] could speak to me.

'Over lunch with Labovitch, I made my position as clear as I could. I was not predisposed to side with Sisu, a hedge fund, but I thought the Ricoh was underperforming and would do better in the private sector, but a reasonable offer would have to be on the table if I was to get involved.

'I thought the rent was too high and that the council ought to get rid.

'If they had something sensible to say, I might well be on their side. But the Ricoh represented a substantial taxpayer investment and the community were entitled to see some return.'

He added: 'I then asked and met Joy Seppala, the decision maker in my view. She came to my House of Commons office with Tim Fisher, Mark Labovitch and Rajay Naik. I made it clear that if she thought I was going to take on my friends, my council and my community for a hedge fund, I wasn't.

'I said, "make an offer that I can support. If a straightforward cash offer is difficult for whatever reason, make a clear proposition on a way forward, something solid you can take to the bank, as the Yanks say."

'I thought the meeting broke up with her agreeing to do this but, despite further exchanges of letters, I never got the kind of clear proposal I was hoping for.

'After that, I decided that Sisu were not an organisation I wanted to have anything to do with.'

I asked more about his view that the Ricoh Arena should be sold and that the council should not be involved in its operation.

He said: 'After the Ricoh was built and, to my mind, was not fulfilling its potential I asked officers and members of the council, "are you open in principal to selling this?" It's not the job of local government to run football stadiums. That's not what people pay their taxes for.

'I was in favour of getting rid, and thought the council would be in a stronger position in the developing row with the club if they made a statement that they were willing to sell to the right people at the right price. But they were totally opposed.

'For John Mutton [then council leader] and George Duggins [then deputy leader], it seemed to me that selling was not up for debate.

'I said to a number of councillors that if they wanted someone to invest real money in the football club, that kind of person would want to own the whole train set. Nobody would invest millions to become a partner of the council.

'Tony Blair's big breakthrough in the Northern Ireland peace process was when he said 'Britain has no strategic interest in maintaining power in Northern Ireland, it's up to the people.'

'That brought a lot of momentum toward peace. He was saying "we, Britain, don't need to own this forever."'

'They could have made a statement which said they were not adamant about retaining ownership of the Ricoh, that it was about what's good for the economy and the football club. We are prepared to sell on the right terms.

'With some members of the council, asking them to sell was like asking Gollum to give up the ring.

'You can understand it in some ways. They had seen it come up out of the ground.'

One strange twist of the internal wrangling going on between the club and ACL came in May 2013 and saw the club's groundsman, John Ledwidge, defect to the stadium firm from the club after funding for pitch maintenance had been pulled by the Sky Blues, who continued to insist they wouldn't need the stadium or the playing surface for the 2013/14 campaign.

ACL, however, seemingly still believed the club would return in time for the new season.

A statement from the stadium company said: 'We're really pleased that John has agreed to join us. He's already worked alongside us for several years, so this was a natural move for both John and the ACL team.

'The pitch is a key asset and feature of the Ricoh Arena and we have set money aside to ensure it is in prime condition come the start of the football season in August.

'When that time arrives, we hope very much that the Sky Blues will be playing on the turf John's going to be in charge of maintaining in the weeks and months ahead, here at their rightful home at the Ricoh Arena in the city of Coventry.'

But Tim Fisher continued to accuse ACL of slamming the Ricoh Arena door in the club's face.

In May 2013, he told the *Coventry Telegraph*: 'ACL refused to negotiate a sensible exit strategy – effectively a longer version of the three-game deal we did last season.'

He added: 'We believe the conduct of the council was motivated not by what was in the best interests of the club but by a desire to wrest control of the club from Sisu.

'By providing state aid, any incentive for ACL to accept a market rate for the club's use of the stadium has disappeared and this has led directly to the club moving to its own stadium.'

In June 2013, ACL made an offer that seemingly could not be refused. Stadium bosses said the club could continue to play at the Ricoh Arena without rent and in exchange for costs being covered.

A statement released by ACL said: 'The directors of Arena Coventry Limited have been deeply concerned with how the emotions of Coventry City Football Club supporters have been tested over recent months and more especially the past few weeks.

'These concerns were discussed in great detail at an ACL Board Meeting on 7 June 2013, and we have today notified the Football League and the joint administrators of a proposed solution for the coming season.

'To enable the football club to fulfil its commitments under Football League regulations, and to provide stability whilst Coventry City Football Club Limited, which owns the league share, remains in administration, ACL has agreed to allow the club to play its home games free of any rental fee, therefore removing any need for the supporters to travel outside the city to watch home games.

'All charges incurred on match day as a consequence of staging a football match will be passed through at cost, for example, stewarding, policing, utilities, frost protection, match day repairs to stadium, health, safety and compliance management and certification, service charges for maintenance contracts e.g. flood lights, generators etc.

'Whilst these sums may vary depending on attendances, it should be noted that policing, stewarding and pitch maintenance have historically been directly managed and paid for by the club.

'ACL also acknowledges that service-related charges can be verified if necessary by an independent external party.

'Given ACL wishes to ensure it provides the best playing surface possible for all football league matches, it will now take direct responsibility for future management and maintenance of the pitch.

'The directors of ACL hope the supporters of Coventry City Football Club, the joint administrators and the Football League will view this as a positive and productive move, and should assist in dispelling the uncertainty and upset of the past weeks.'

But the deal was flatly rejected by the club. Quite why has never really been explained, although access to stadium revenues was a repeated sticking point during this period.

It would be the first of many opportunities for a return to be dismissed.

In the context of the court judgments which covered this period, it would be easy to conclude that withdrawing the club's business from the Ricoh Arena completely was yet another attempt to distress ACL with a view to securing a stake in the firm at a reduced rate.

During this time, Tim Fisher was asked by the *Coventry Telegraph:* 'Have your business tactics over the past year been designed to bankrupt ACL so you can attempt to wrest control of the Ricoh Arena?'

He said: 'In an attempt to put both the club and ACL on a sound financial footing, we had a series of meetings in 2012 aimed at resolving the financial difficulties facing both parties.

'As part of this, we reached agreement with the council to buy out the ACL debt in return for a half share in the stadium business and extension of ACL's lease to 125 years, which means it remains 100 per cent council-owned. We would just access the revenues, which is crucial.

'This deal was documented, signed by all parties and then reneged on by the council. The council made the problem even worse by then using public funds, something that is now subject to the judicial review proceedings.

'We need to be very clear that this is not about ownership of the freehold in the stadium, which would have continued to be held by the council, with the club taking back the 50 per cent interest in head-leaseholder ACL, which it was always intended to have.

'We believe the conduct of the council was motivated, not by what was in the best interests of the club, but by a desire to wrest control of the club from Sisu.

'We have always wanted this to be a mutually beneficial partnership instead of an outdated agreement that is more likely to lead to mutual self-destruction.'

The Sky Blues were rapidly accelerating on a path which would take them away from their home city. It became apparent the club had made serious enquires about becoming the tenant of another club in the Midlands. The earlier front-runner appeared to be Walsall's Banks's Stadium. But it later emerged the club planned to move to to Northampton's Sixfields Stadium, 35 miles and almost 45 minutes away by car from the Ricoh Arena.

The situation was critical, and the *Coventry Telegraph* acted to voice the concerns of Sky Blues fans everywhere.

The *City Must Stay* campaign was launched alongside a scathing editorial from then-editor Alun Thorne.

It read: 'There are many people to blame for the mess Coventry City is in. Your beloved club has been badly run for years, long before Sisu rescued it from administration and pumped in millions of pounds to keep it afloat.

'But in the end, it is the owners who have decided to take the club out of Coventry and away from its fans.

'Many fans have long called for Sisu to go. Not the *Telegraph*. We have acknowledged it is their investors' cash that has kept the club alive – no matter how badly it has been wasted in taking the club from the Championship to League One.

'But now it is different. Sisu's plan to take your club 35 miles away to Northampton for at least three years while they build a new stadium near, but outside, Coventry is utter madness and will tear the heart out of this city. As a newspaper, we cannot support an owner who is willing to do this.

'It will leave the club – already a shadow of its proud former self – as a sham, a sick joke playing in front of the minority of fans who haven't been alienated by this shameful soap opera. Coventry City have a home. It is in Coventry, not Northampton. It is called the Ricoh Arena. You may wish they were still at Highfield Road but that is long gone.

'ACL have repeated their offer for the club to play at the Ricoh rent free – but paying match day costs – while they are in administration, so there is another option to Sixfields. There must surely still be a chance to find a compromise.

'Whatever the rights and wrongs of the Ricoh row – and let's be clear that neither side are faultless – the argument is almost irrelevant. Coventry City must play in Coventry.

'Manager Steven Pressley said that he wants City to stay in Coventry and that he hoped a solution could be found. We share that view and hope that his bosses can give their bright young manager the fanbase he needs to push his team up the table towards promotion.

'The current owners and custodians have told us that they have to move to safeguard the club's future, that staying at the Ricoh doesn't make financial sense. Fair enough, but more than 14,000 of you have signed our *City Must Stay* petition and the overwhelming majority of supporters at Sky Blues chief executive Tim Fisher's forums told him they wouldn't follow the club outside of Coventry. So what is the club without the fans?

'Under Sisu, City's average crowd in 2008/09 was 17,420. They lost millions of pounds. Gates have fallen every year but the losses have continued to pile up. Last season's average gate was 10,973. Next season we'd guess it will be 2-3,000. Can anyone see the financial sense in that?

'Fans have already started a *Not One Penny More* campaign, vowing not to spend any money with the club until they agree to play home games at the Ricoh Arena.

'Is Northampton still making financial sense?

'Of course, the club knew all of this before yesterday's news about quitting Coventry for Northampton came out. But still they plough on. Mr Fisher has repeatedly said this is not a game of brinkmanship, that they have left the Ricoh for good.

'Well, if Sisu won't keep City in Coventry they should stand aside and let someone else do what is best for the club and its long-suffering supporters.

'Administration has had one benefit for Sky Blues fans. It has shown that there are investors interested in buying the club. If these people are worthy owners of your club, then they must have figured out that they were never likely to be able to pick it up on the cheap from the administrator. They were always going to have to talk to Sisu.

'If you want to buy the Sky Blues, do it now before it's too late. Buy them now before the club is torn away from a generation of fans.

'Pick up the phone and make Joy Seppala an offer. And Joy, thanks for the £45m, the fans should be grateful for that. But if Sisu's plan is truly to take it from the city that bears its name then the time has come to pass on the baton to new owners committed to keeping the Sky Blues where they belong.

'City Must Stay.'

One person to add their backing to the campaign was former Coventry City chairman Peter Robins, the son of legendary Sky Blues chairman Derrick Robins.

Clearly unimpressed by the suggestion the club could be leaving the city, he said: 'What a bizarre and outrageous situation that one should even have to sign a petition.

'What on earth would my father and Jimmy Hill, who built this club, have to say?

'I don't think I could put into words what dad would have said. He wouldn't have let it get to this stage in the first place but he would have been absolutely outraged that the club that he built with Jimmy is behaving in this bizarre and outrageous way. He'd be totally mortified.

'I feel that my father's legacy is being destroyed. He built an outstanding success and that has been destroyed over many years. I find it staggering.'

Despite a total of about 15,000 supporters eventually signing the petition to support the campaign, club officials stuck to their guns.

Supporters continued to push Tim Fisher for answers over the breakdown of talks with ACL designed to reach a compromise on rent and a share of match day revenues.

He said: 'We realised that the business was nothing short of appalling.'

He added that the decision to launch a judicial review of the city council's decision to buy out ACL's debt from Yorkshire Bank was '£100,000 well spent'.

He said: 'The cost of legals is way more than £100,000 and it's travelling northwards at a rate of knots. What about the £100,000 the council will have spent on this? How many jobs would that have saved?

'The council are closing this centre and that centre, closing old people's homes. I'm not sure that adds up.

'The council have lost control of the situation and will do anything they can to stop the club moving on. The judicial review is very clear.

'The claimant says that the defendants worked against the best interests of the club, worked in bad faith, tried to wrest control of the club.'

Little did Mr Fisher know at the time that the initial £100,000 was just the tip of the iceberg. Three years on, the legal battle continues and is now estimated to have cost well over £1m.

Mr Fisher also revealed that the Football League had given them a list of grounds they would approve as a temporary home.

He said: 'At the moment, we are sharpening the pencil on the final agreement.'

He admitted that it was a commercial risk and that crowds would slump 'between 6-7,000 if the team does really well, as low as 3,000 if it doesn't.'

Mr Fisher said: 'The numbers don't look great but there is a real risk that this football club spirals down and down.

'Unless you get to a sustainable model, there is no way this club will ever pick up. Why else would we do it?'

The estimation of crowds between 6-7,000 proved to be well wide of the mark, as did another prediction made by the club's chief executive.

That summer, he told Coventry City London Supporters Club that 'Sisu is a distressed debt fund and therefore batters people in court'.

For those of you keeping score, the hedge fund drew 0-0 with the charity and suffered a heavy defeat to Coventry City Council before losing again in a replay. At the time of writing, it's seeking yet another replay.

On 8 July 2013, the news all Coventry City fans dreaded was finally confirmed. The Football League had rubber-stamped an application for the Sky Blues to ground share at Northampton's Sixfields Stadium for three years – with an option for a further two years. The club had also been forced to pay a £1m bond as an assurance that they would return to Coventry.

Announcing the news, Football League chairman, Greg Clarke, said: 'The Football League believes that clubs should play in the towns and cities from which they take their name.

Nonetheless, from time to time, the board is asked to consider temporary relocations as a means for securing a club's ongoing participation in our competition.

'With no prospect of an agreement being reached between Otium and ACL, the board was placed in an unenviable position, with the very real possibility of Coventry City being unable to fulfil its fixtures for next season. This would inevitably call into question the club's continued membership of the Football League.

'The board did not take this decision lightly and it remains a matter of deep regret that the two parties involved cannot come to an agreement.

'I urge both Otium and ACL to continue to explore every possible opportunity to resolve this dispute for the good of the City of Coventry, its football club and people living in the local community.'

Tim Fisher welcomed the news on behalf of the club, saying: 'We are very pleased that the Football League has found our plans acceptable.

'Nobody wanted this day to come, but we feel we have no choice but to take this course of action and that the only credible future for the club now lies in owning its own stadium.

'Building a stadium that is ours in the Coventry area, and which will generate revenues we can put on the field of play is necessary to ensure the club can succeed under the FIFA fair play rules.

'If there had been an economic option which would have allowed us to stay at the Ricoh, we would have pursued it. There was no proposal on the table in time for us to make realistic plans for the coming season. We could not wait any longer.

'Over the last month or so – through a series of forums – we have made it clear this move is not a game of brinkmanship or a negotiating strategy, it is the only credible option. If our plans did not show a clear path for returning to the Coventry City area, they would not have been approved by the league.'

Speaking about the deal, Northampton chairman David Cardoza said: 'This helps out a fellow club who came to us and asked for our assistance and it is a much-needed additional revenue stream for Northampton Town Football Club.

'We totally understand that the majority of Coventry fans feel their club should be playing in their city and we are sorry they are not, but the issues about whether or not they could use the Ricoh or any other venue in Coventry are not ours to discuss.

'Coventry City Football Club felt the only option was to move outside of the city, and our first involvement in this process was when we were approached by Coventry City asking us to help a fellow football club. There wasn't any plan for us to try and tempt another club away from their local community for our financial gain.

'We are simply helping a fellow football club at their request.'

James Whiting, who was then financial director at Northampton, revealed how the move had come about.

He said: 'The arrangement we had for Coventry to play here; they obviously came to us as a club needing to have somewhere to play – and in a very short period of time because of the issues they were facing at the time.

'We had to come to an agreement with them on that and we didn't really have an opinion as to whether it was right or wrong.

'We saw it as being better that the club has somewhere to play than not at all.

'We wanted to help out a fellow club.

'From the time the deal was signed, all the games that Coventry City played here, the impact on us was minimal.

'Really, they rocked up into town on the day, played their games and disappeared.

'From our staff and supporters' point of view, there was very little impact, to the point that you wouldn't really notice they were here.'

Ricoh Arena bosses did not take the announcement lightly. They immediately launched a legal threat to Northampton Town FC, accusing the club of essentially luring their tenants away and causing damage to their business.

The action was subsequently dropped after Mr Cardoza insisted the Cobblers 'would not be bullied' by the stadium firm.

I asked ACL director Peter Knatchbull-Hugessen if, three years on, he regretted that the stadium firm had taken that action.

He said: 'It wasn't unfair on Northampton. It is what you do in business. It was a strategy to protect our interests.

'You are stuck as a director to see someone damaging your company financially, and you have lawyers saying this is what you should be doing to recover that business.'

The day after the ground-share deal was announced, suspended life president Joe Elliott announced he would resign his position.

He told me: 'I resigned as life president because I didn't agree with our beloved Sky Blues being taken out of the city it plays in.

'It wasn't a difficult decision. When the Gary Hoffman Chinese takeover attempt came up in 2011, Ken Dulieu [then CCFC chairman] asked me to resign and then I was suspended.

'When they went to Sixfields, I thought that is it and I resigned. I wouldn't go to Sixfields but I would attend all the away matches.

'My emotions as a fan during the time were just very sad. I was upset I could not go and watch my team, along with many other supporters.

'I couldn't believe it, I never thought it would get to that point.'

What can only be described as panic began to takeover the Coventry City fan base. This was a distressing time for many supporters of the club – many of whom had a financial and emotional connection with the Ricoh Arena.

There was the memorial garden at the stadium where the ashes of deceased Sky Blues fans had been scattered.

And, as the stadium was being built, many supporters had paid for bricks bearing their names or the names of loved ones to be placed in the walls of the stadium building. With the passage of time, some of these Sky Blues supporters had also passed away.

Now there was a threat that the only remaining connection these supporters had with their club was about to be ripped away. It was nothing short of harrowing.

Then, another ray of hope emerged as former vice-chairman Gary Hoffman made an offer to cover the club's rent.

He said: 'My proposal is this: I raise the money to pay the rent for the next three seasons. I assume £400,000 per season as that is the number speculated

'Otium has to pay nothing towards it. They save the costs of the deal on Northampton, excluding any break clause costs, which we would pay too.

'ACL get their rent. The casino benefits, the hotel benefits. In fact, everyone benefits. No losers

'I assume that the attendance at the Ricoh would be at least 5,000 per game more than at Sixfields. This is undoubtedly conservative. So, 5,000 at an average £15 per ticket for 25 games. £1.875m extra revenue. Otium can take half of this upside for trading purposes. The people who put the money up with me would take a return to cover financing and other costs. But kept to a reasonable sum. The rest should be invested in the academy.

'Forget the long term for the time being. If Otium want to build a new stadium, that is up to them.'

But the offer was apparently rejected out of hand by Sisu. Club officials suggested the deal wasn't as good as it was presented and that there were charges which could be levied depending on attendance targets being reached and other similar clauses.

On 20 July 2013, there was one of the greatest displays of Sky Blue unity in the club's history.

Hundreds were expected, but thousands stood shoulder to shoulder as Coventry City supporters marched on the city centre in protest at the decision to allow the club to leave its home city.

The march was organised by supporters' group the Sky Blue Trust and attracted an estimated 5,000 people who marched from the site of the original home of the club, Gosford Green, to Broadgate in the city centre.

There were scenes the likes of which have not been seen for a generation as Coventry supporters turned the streets Sky Blue and ground the city centre to a halt.

The last time Coventry witnessed anything similar was when the club lifted the FA Cup in 1987, but fans were now taking to the streets for a very different reason.

It was a rare moment of pride and passion the likes of which would be few and far between for many supporters over the coming months.

Jan Mokrzycki, spokesman for The Sky Blue Trust, explained the success of the march was in the sense of unity it provided at a time when Coventry City's fanbase had been split and grown weary after months of hyperbole and arguments which had damaged the reputation of their club and put its future in jeopardy.

He said: 'It was just one of those ideas that evolved from a brainstorming session.

'The night before, we had a meeting with the police and we didn't know whether we were going to get 20, 200 or 2,000. The police thought we would get about 500.

'The next day we were standing in Gosford Green and we were just absolutely astonished as people kept on coming. It was just brilliant. It proved the club wasn't dead.

'It was a chance to show that the people of Coventry cared about the football club and send a message to all of those involved in taking our club out of the city.

'This had never happened before; a club being taken out of their city over a rent dispute.

'It was the fans who were going to suffer.

'But at the time, most people thought "surely they can't mean it' and that it would not happen."

He added: 'I think the march was a real positive. People were divided over who was to blame, whether to go and so on, while others just wanted to watch their team.

'This march united them all. They all wanted the team to be kept in Coventry. Football is a way of uniting people. It unites people of different religions, people from different ethnic backgrounds, people with different political beliefs.

'That day showed that people of all backgrounds were united in their love of the Sky Blue shirt.

'The numbers were overwhelming. Everybody who took part that day should be proud.'

But club officials remained unmoved in their stance that the club must leave Coventry.

Speaking after the march, Tim Fisher said: 'We completely understand the frustration and the passion that was shown at the march. I have seen it each time I have met supporters at forums or individually. It is a position I have unequivocal respect for.

'Our fans do not want us to ground-share but it is not an option we have pursued lightly or with any relish. The decision was taken to ensure we could fulfil our fixtures and safeguard the future of the club.'

Political pressure to prevent the move continued through Bob Ainsworth MP, who again brought the issue to the attention of Parliament with just days to go until the club kicked off the season 35 miles away from Coventry.

He revealed a letter from Andy Williamson, the Football League's chief operating officer, which defended the decision to allow the Sky Blues to leave their home city.

The letter read: 'In order to keep the club alive, the Football League board agreed to offer the Otium Entertainment

Group the club's share in the Football League, providing it accepted various entry conditions, including a commitment that it meet the financial offer made to creditors under the proposed CVA.'

It stated the league, in considering whether to allow the Northampton ground-share, was placed in an 'unenviable position as a consequence of a commercial dispute between the club and its landlord'.

It added: 'The league understands this situation has caused great distress for many supporters of Coventry City... We will now continue with our endeavours to get the club playing in its home city at the earliest opportunity, though this will be against a backdrop of the club having had ten points deducted for failing to achieve a CVA due to the actions of its former landlord.

'For the record, it is categorically not the case that the Football League has failed to apply its own rules as the board retains the right to permit clubs to move ground at its discretion.'

Bob Ainsworth told me he was unimpressed by the Football League during the entire length of this saga, dissatisfaction which had begun when he summoned top officials to Westminster in a bid to prevent the move to Northampton.

He said: 'I arranged a meeting with the Football League at the House of Commons. I had also had lots of written exchanges with them.

'The meeting was in the summer just before they went to play at Sixfields.

'At that meeting, Paul Harris [Alan Higgs Charity trustee] produced an offer of lower rent and asked them to take it to Sisu.

'Sean Harvey [chief executive of the Football League] was there and they also had a secretary and a lawyer.

'The Football League backed the club that the rent was too high. But I felt they were pretty weak and, with the offer, had hoped they would do more.

'They were basically saying, "can't you do something about this?"'

But it appeared nobody could do anything about it and on Sunday 11 August at 3pm, Coventry City Football Club played its first 'home' game outside of its home city – 35 miles away in Northampton. It was an unforgivable betrayal of the club's illustrious and proud history in the eyes of the vast majority of Coventry City supporters.

The sense of repulsion was underlined by a paltry attendance of just 2,204 – just 908 of whom were Coventry supporters. That figure would almost exactly represent the average crowd the club could expect during its time at Sixfields. So much for the 6,000–7,000 per game Mr Fisher had confidently predicted just weeks earlier.

Chapter 11
Jimmy's Hill

THE day Coventry City played their first game at Sixfields, many fans were left with a strange sense of loss and emptiness.

It was made all the more surreal by the fact a team of Sky Blues legends were lining up for a charity match at the Ricoh Arena, which got under way shortly before Coventry kicked off against Bristol City for the club's first 'home' fixture in Northampton.

The charity match, organised to celebrate the 130th anniversary of Coventry City Former Players' Association (CCFPA), had become an unofficial protest for Sky Blues fans to express their discontent at the switch to Sixfields.

Billy Bell, vice-chairman of the CCFPA and organiser of the fixture, said: 'It was never done deliberately as a confrontation, but now the people of Coventry will vote with their feet.

'We're hoping for a large, large crowd to show the football world that Coventry people are not happy with what is going on at our club.'

And people did vote with their feet as just 908 Coventry City supporters attended the club's first game at Sixfields compared with more than 7,000 who attended the Ricoh and enjoyed the nostalgia of seeing the likes of Darren Huckerby, Noel Whelan and Terry Gibson perform in Sky Blue once again.

But it was bitter-sweet for Coventry fans, who felt they had no choice but to stay away from Sixfields.

Those who did decide to attend were able to feast on football excitement as City edged out Bristol 5-4 in a thrilling encounter.

Alan Poole, of the *Coventry Telegraph*, summed up the events of that day.

He said: 'By universal consent, this was one of the saddest days in the history of Coventry City. But against the odds and pretty much all expectations, it threw up one of the most exhilarating matches their supporters have witnessed in those 130 years of spectacular highs and lows.

'Leading 3-0 at the interval, the City youngsters' self-belief was sapped by two streaky goals and they were unaccountably pegged back to 3-3 when new recruit Andy Webster blemished his impressive debut with a glaring, ring-rusty error.

'Having regained their advantage inside a minute, they suddenly found themselves at 4-4 with 15 minutes to play. But they again responded instantaneously and then held their nerve through an agonising added-time period that was scheduled for six minutes and stretched to nearly eight.'

He added: 'It's clear that however people choose to support Coventry City this season, they're in for a hair-raising ride.

'It will certainly stretch their nerves to the limit – how unbearably, inexcusably sad that they are being forced to question their lifelong loyalties.'

In conversations with supporters, the sense of sadness was repeatedly summed up to me by likening the disappearance of the Sky Blues to Northampton to that of the death of a relative. The pain and anguish Coventry City fans felt during this period was very real. It was completely unforgivable that it had come to this.

Fans dealt with the situation in different ways, but it impacted them all and the hurt they felt was very real.

One Sky Blues fan vowed to go on a 24-hour hunger strike every time Coventry City played a 'home' match away from the Ricoh Arena next season.

Nigel Warren insisted he'd rather go hungry than watch his beloved team in action outside the city limits.

He told the *Coventry Telegraph*: 'Football and the Sky Blues are my life – I eat, drink and sleep it – so if they take my club away from the Ricoh, I will not eat for the 24 hours of each and every home game.

'It may sound silly but what Sisu and Tim Fisher are planning really hurts.

'The fans are really annoyed and disgusted at the way we are being treated and maybe something like this will make the club sit up and listen.'

For those fans who did decide to follow the team to Sixfields, it was obviously a painstaking decision.

One such supporter, who decided to renew his season ticket despite the move, was Alan Payne, who has been a supporter since the mid-1950s and is a former Coventry shareholder.

He said: 'The Sixfields period was, without any question at all, the worst thing I have ever seen at the club.

'I've heard people say before they are not going because of this player or that manager and this felt like an extension of that. Before the season started, I was really beating myself up in terms of what to do.

'I prepared myself to go to the charity game with the former players at the Ricoh Arena, but I had followed the club all over the country and the players who were there at the time, it wasn't their fault.

'I thought "I support Coventry City Football Club" and I ended up buying my ticket two days before the first game at Sixfields.

'I felt I had to continue to follow the football club. 'Unfortunately, that was at Northampton. I hated going there.

The first three or four matches had a large feeling of guilt. But when the players came out on the pitch, I just felt like I was watching my football team.

'I felt guilty because the majority of people felt it was wrong to go to Sixfields.

'I have been a member of the Sky Blue Trust for many years and the majority of the members there, and the majority of fans, thought it was wrong to go.

'I want Sisu to go probably more than anyone. But I was always of the opinion, even before we went there, that the only way we would get new owners was to support the football club in large numbers and make it a more tangible prospect. I don't see Sisu just walking away.

'Most people had the view that it was up to the individual whether they went or stayed away.

'You had to decide for yourself, but the people I knew who shouted the loudest and had the strongest opinions were the ones who felt the only way to get rid of Sisu was to ignore them and not give them any money. I felt the total opposite.

'But I could never forgive Sisu for what they did to my club. To me, that was an unforgivable act.'

Asked if the low crowds and the 70-mile round trip ever put him off attending, he said: 'I was behind the goal and if you had 100 people there, that was it. After a while, you would recognise quite a lot of those 100 people.

'The people I spoke to had a similar sort of feeling to me. They were still our football team.

'Although we weren't happy to be there, it was still Coventry City Football Club.

'One game, the groundsman turned to us and said "I don't know why you don't like coming here, the football is great!"

'He was right, the football there was fantastic. You have to give credit to the players at the time.

'But it never felt like home. Our home was still the Ricoh.'

He added: 'My wife used to say, "that's just you, it's just what you do." I used to drive and it didn't take very long.

'Some of my closest friends who used to go wouldn't travel to Sixfields and they still haven't gone back to this day. They won't while the current owners are there.

'But I said I just wanted to support my football team. We don't talk about football any more, which is a shame, but we haven't fallen out or anything like that.'

Some fans expressed their frustration by attending at arms length – taking up position on a hill behind one of the goals at Northampton's ground. That hill became affectionately known as 'Jimmy's Hill' by those who decided to make it their permanent base.

Alan said: 'I used to walk across the bottom of the hill and I could see the people up there. For the first few games, I couldn't bring myself to look at them. I had this feeling of guilt about doing it.

'After I had been to a few games I did look up at them but, because I was in the stand that backed on to the hill, once I was in the ground I couldn't hear or see them.

'The first game there was people saying, "don't go in with signs and things", but we never had any sort of abuse or anything like that directed at us.'

One of the ringleaders of 'The Hillers', as some referred to them, was Sky Blue Trust chairman Steve Brown. The supporters on the hill formed a special bond and earned the respect of many for enduring all types of weather in order to make their feelings about the move to Sixfields known.

He told me: 'I was on the hill at Northampton and I'm proud to have been one of only two people who went to every single game.

'We probably averaged 20 to 25, but we had 250 for one game, and there was always at least ten to 15 of us.

'We tried to make as much noise as we could because some people used to say they couldn't hear us.

'We had a World War II siren and we must have got through about three drums. We even had a double decker bus to bring people over for some matches.

'It was so cold some nights. My wife used to make me a flask of coffee to get me through it.'

He added: 'I never thought we would actually end up at Sixfields. I thought it was just all pie-in-the-sky nonsense. I didn't think it would ever happen and I didn't believe they ever had any intention of it actually happening.

'The day it was confirmed, I got a phone call saying they were moving to Northampton. Straight away, a group of us jumped in our cars and headed to Northampton to take part in the first demonstration against the move.

'I was disappointed and really angry that we had left the Ricoh Arena, which was built for us. It was not a nice feeling.

'We all had every intention of demonstrating for the first couple of games. It was pretty obvious they had this hill, so we decided to protest on there for a couple of games. Then it just became a habit.'

But there was obvious division among fans. Some supporters adopted a *Not One Penny More* stance, feeling the best way to force a return was to cut off the club's income by non-attendance. Others believed the best method was to support the club and make the business strong enough for Sisu to be able to sell it as an attractive proposition.

Steve said: 'We had a lot of hassle. We were abused literally every game.

'As people were going in, they would ask us why aren't we going in. They said we were killing the club.

'Some people would stand on the bottom of the hill and shout abuse. It was very sad and it will take a while to get over it for some fans.

'At the time, I was disappointed in those who were going in. At first, I was really angry because I thought if nobody went in it would be over really quickly.

'But then you hear from people who want their kids to watch Coventry City or didn't want to get involved in the politics and just wanted to watch their team – and I can understand that now. But at the time, it felt like they were scabs. I was on the hill then, and I would do it again if they ever went back. But I won't knock anybody who went in.'

He added that the actions of protesters inevitably caused some division between the Sky Blue Trust and the club.

'The reason the club fell out with the Sky Blue Trust was that we had been asked to support the move by Tim Fisher, but 99.9 per cent of our members said they were against it,' he said.

'We could not back Tim Fisher. They accused us of not helping the club. But we felt if we just walked away, this thing would slowly kill the club. We had to make a statement.'

The vast majority of supporters simply could not bring themselves to make the trip to Sixfields, even if they could avoid entering the ground itself by taking refuge on the hill.

It was the biggest boycott of an English team by its supporters since Wimbledon had been allowed to relocate from London to Milton Keynes in 2003.

During the 2013/14 season, the average attendance at 'home' matches for Coventry would be 2,364 – the Football League's fourth lowest, above only Accrington Stanley, Dagenham & Redbridge and Morecambe, all in League Two.

That represented a drop of 78 per cent from the average of 10,938 attracted by the club in the previous season at the Ricoh Arena and emphasised the strength of feeling among the club's supporters.

The home attendances were the lowest in the club's Football League history – surpassed only during the team's Birmingham League days of 1905/06. The club hit rock bottom during a midweek game in February 2014, when only 1,603 attended the Carlisle game. It was the lowest league crowd in the club's Football League history.

But the support was clearly still there, with the Sky Blue Army's average away game attendance rocketing by 25 per cent in the same period – up from 6,895 to 8,651.

One of the stay-away supporters was Daniel Gill, who had held a season ticket every season since the 1991/92 campaign. But that all changed in 2013.

He said: 'I had been a season ticket holder since I was six and could count on one hand the number of home games I had missed since the 1991/92 season.

'I started going with my dad and granddad and have always been with my dad.

'The decision not to buy a season ticket was tough. It was what we had been doing my whole life. It was my life.

'But we could not support or agree with what was happening – picking up the club and moving them more than 30 miles just to score points in an argument.

'It was hard to decide not to buy a season ticket in some ways, but looking at the facts it was actually pretty easy.

'Nobody actually thought it would happen. We had heard all the quotes and interviews but even when the march happened I don't think anybody believed it would actually happen.

'It wasn't until the first game of the season that I actually believed it. That's when it was real.

'I respect the decisions of everyone who did go. It was difficult for everybody.

'It divided City fans. There was a horrible split between people who were going and people who would not go. It was terrible division and I would say it is still there to a certain extent. I don't think the fanbase has ever fully recovered.

'It's definitely still in my mind. I don't think I can ever forgive everyone involved for what happened. A lot of people probably feel the same, especially while there's still uncertainty over the future.'

He added: 'It was hard to fill the void. It was what I had been doing since I was a child. I would stay close to the radio or go out shopping. But it was strange.

'Anger was really the overriding emotion at the time. Everyone involved in the argument – at the club, ACL and the council – had let it get to the point where it actually happened.

'I would say it was fair to compare the sense of loss to that of losing a loved one. It was a real empty feeling that something

I had since I was so young, and was a huge part of my life, had been taken away from me by other people's decisions.

'It could have been avoided. Egos and individual characters took over and the fans just got completely forgotten about.'

One of the most striking shows of unity among Coventry City supporters came in the form of a sort of guerilla protest involving large amounts of Sky Blue ribbons and lots of willing volunteers.

Hundreds of ribbons were put up on prominent buildings across the city centre, including Coventry Cathedral, the Council House and the *Coventry Telegraph*. Major routes were also lined with the ribbons as supporters undertook one of the most visually striking protests of the entire saga.

The 'Tie A Sky Blue Ribbon' initiative was aimed at drawing attention to the fans' plight and was based around a 1973 chart-topping single *Tie A Yellow Ribbon Round the Ole Oak Tree* by the band Dawn, which highlights a convention in some countries to tie a yellow ribbon around an oak tree when a loved one is away for a prolonged period of time.

Some mischievous campaigners even plastered the club's Ryton training ground with the ribbons and wrote 'Sisu Out' on the gates in ribbon before it was hastily removed by club officials.

Even the London headquarters of Sisu and the Football League got the ribbon treatment as supporters found increasingly inventive ways to voice their displeasure.

Such was the almost poetic nature of the expressions of pain and anguish felt by City supporters that one documentary maker decided to produce an artistic record of what had occurred during the team's spell at Sixfields.

Duncan Whitley created the piece called *Not A Penny More: the Benefactress' Tale*, which told the story through images and music alone. The dreamlike piece was supposed to give the impression that the saga was being seen through the eyes of a time-travelling Lady Godiva.

He explained: 'It's about football fans and the football movement. It's about how football is becoming more and more out of reach of the people whose heritage it is.

'It's also about faith. I see a lot of faith in the group known as The Hillers who went to every game in Northampton come rain or shine. To me, that's real faith.'

But it wasn't just supporters who were suffering from the situation. Those who played a direct role in creating the club's illustrious history spoke out against what they saw as a direct betrayal of the club's heritage.

One such player was Ronnie Farmer, the former City midfielder once voted as the club's greatest ever player. He had played for the Sky Blues in all four divisions in the 1950s and 1960s and still lives in Tile Hill.

With tears in his eyes, the then 78-year-old told me he feared he may never see his beloved Sky Blues play again.

He said: 'I was sad when we left Highfield Road and now I wish we had never left. The situation at the club is a farce.

'At my age I have realised I may never get to see them play again. It makes me very sad.

'I used to go to games but I won't go to Northampton because I class that team as Northampton reserves. It is not a Coventry team if they are not playing in Coventry.'

Another former player who boycotted games was former defender Dietmar Bruck.

The then 69-year-old said: 'It is frustrating and annoying that we have two different groups who are behaving like kids and won't negotiate. They are like little babies.

'The worrying part about all this is that, because it is going on so long, people are finding other things to do instead of watching Coventry City and we are going to lose generations of supporters.

'There's no way, as an ex-player, I will go to Northampton.'

Former Northern Irish winger Willie Humphries, who was Jimmy Hill's first signing in 1962, said: 'It is very sad to see where they are now.

'When I left Coventry City and went back to Northern Ireland, the first result I would always look for was Coventry's.

'I was very upset to hear they had moved out of the city and the sooner they get back to Coventry, the better.'

Unfortunately for Willie, and the thousands of Coventry City supporters who had decided to stay away, it would be some time before the Sky Blues would be back where they belonged.

Chapter 12

Theatre of broken dreams

C OVENTRY City being unceremoniously ripped from the heart of their community and dumped into the less-than-glamorous surroundings of Sixfields clearly had a massive impact on the supporters.

But how did going from playing in the impressive surroundings of the Ricoh Arena to the home of then League Two Northampton Town impact the team?

Players and management understandably toed the party line at the time of the Sixfields saga. But many have since moved on to new clubs and, with the passage of time, have decided they are able to talk more openly about what was one of the most turbulent periods in the clubs history.

The man tasked with gluing the team together was then manager Steven Pressley, who had replaced Mark Robins as manager less than six months before the ground-share deal was struck.

Speaking about the build-up to the Sixfields move, he said: 'Before I took over, when I first met with them to discuss the position of management, there were whispers then that there could be problems in regards to the lease of the Ricoh Arena.

'In discussions then, I was aware that there was an outstanding issue with that.

'Although it was not definite we would be moving away, they were quite transparent prior to me coming that there was the possibility of a breakdown between the club and ACL.

'I always hoped it would be resolved. The last thing you want as a manger, going into a new environment and coming down to England for the first time, is having to deal with some of the issues we had to deal with.

'We were always in hope it would never come to what it did.

'It was far from ideal. Initially, there had been talk of us moving to Walsall. That looked a more likely option in the early stages, but that fell through.

'The Northampton situation arose and it wasn't what we wanted. But the reality was my coaching staff and I had to put on our brave faces to ensure we didn't create a negative environment going there.

'The most important thing for us was, in that particular season with what we had to endure, surviving in the league – and the survival of the club.

'We had to appear reasonably positive, but the reality was it was far from ideal.'

There was a feeling among many Coventry City supporters that, perversely, playing in front of reduced crowds at Sixfields might actually have benefited City's young squad, especially as the team started the 2013/14 season well. Pressley agreed there was a degree of truth in that.

He said: 'Initially, in the summer months when the pitch was good and there was a good feeling when the sun was shining, the reality of the situation was not as severe.

'I also think the squad was very young at the time. In regards to the performances of some of our younger players, there was maybe not the same degree of pressure playing at Northampton than there was playing at the Ricoh –

especially when we were blooding so many young players at the time.

'Even if you look at the bench at the time – in fact some of them made appearances – some of them are no longer involved in football at any level.

'The situation was reliant on so many young players, and probably playing at Northampton took a degree of pressure away from them. In hindsight, it was maybe easier to blood them.

'But the reality was, once the honeymoon period of the summer months passed by, running out on a cold rainy January in front of just over 1,000 supporters is far from ideal.'

Having joined a club which boasted the Ricoh Arena as its home, only to see it descend into turmoil and engulfed by a toxic atmosphere fuelled by animosity over the move to Sixfields, it would be easy to understand if the manager had seriously considered walking away at any point. But he insisted that it never crossed his mind.

He said: 'Never, never, never – and we had to endure some remarkable situations.

'But what we did try to do was keep a degree of normality about playing there.

'We didn't turn up on a bus for home games. Probably firstly because finances wouldn't have allowed it, but secondly we felt that if the players reported in their own cars there would be a degree of it feeling a little bit like a home game.

'Small things like that we tried to keep in place, and the staff at Northampton were fantastic with us. They were very welcoming.

'The small things we could influence were positive, but it was never ideal. You couldn't really train with real intensity around the stadium because there was never a big enough support there to do so.'

Asked if the move from the Ricoh Arena had impacted the ability to attract players to the club, or retain them, Pressley said: 'Without doubt the Leon Clarke situation, had we been playing at the Ricoh, had our finances been in a better position, they're the types of players we possibly could have retained.

'But when you have a club like Wolves come knocking, and they're paying the money they were, playing in front of 20,000 supporters, then it's difficult to convince these types of players to stay.

'In my first season, I wasn't really in a position where I could really attract anybody anyway because we were under a transfer embargo.

'In terms of attracting them to play at Northampton in my first season, it didn't have a great effect.

'The players we could sign in my first season, the reality was, were players not attached to football clubs after the transfer window had closed.

'The second season, without doubt, the attraction to bring in certain players was affected.

'I'm not going to name any players, I think that would be wrong. But what I will say is that there were a number of important players that we did try and bring in and there was no doubt that was an issue to them.

'And not just an issue to them. The other issue was financially we couldn't compete with many of the bigger clubs in the league.

'Coventry are regarded as a big club, but financially we weren't against some of the other clubs you would consider to be top clubs in that league. We couldn't compete financially because the Northampton budget dictated that.'

Pressley has been quoted in the press since his departure suggesting that the club would not exist if he hadn't taken some of the actions he took during the club's time in Northampton.

Asked to elaborate on that issue, he said: 'I had to reduce the budget. They talk now about for the first time the club is able to work within its means.

'Well, it's no coincidence that I reduced the budget by 60 per cent during my time in charge. I blooded all the young players.

'When I look at the situation, one of my frustrations is my remit was a certain remit and I look from afar now and the remit has completely changed.

'That's the difficulty within football. When you're asked to do a certain thing, you do it for the longevity of the football club.

'The football club can't deviate when a manager leaves from what it's set out to do.

'The plan was a five-year plan. That was for me to go in, transform the academy, bring through and develop our young players, reduce the playing budget by a considerable margin to get us to become a sustainable business, and at the same time get results on a Saturday.

'Now if you put all those things together, it's a big task. For a big percentage of the time, we managed to do that.

'But the reality was we needed to sell certain players at certain moments.

'We needed to sell Callum Wilson, there's no doubt about that. The club survived that season on the sale of Callum Wilson. A brief thing, but hugely important to the club moving forward.

'We made enormous sacrifices and these are the types of things that can be overlooked.

'My decisions at times were not always long-term, we also had to make short-term decisions like the Callum Wilson one to see the club survive over a turbulent period.'

With bitter court battles, vociferous protests and continued talk of possible new stadiums or a return the Ricoh Arena, there were plenty of distractions off the field during the Sixfields saga.

Asked if this ever affected the players or management, Pressley said: 'The one thing is we're not blind to it. We're aware of the whole situation.

'The fact of the matter is, as a manager, you want to manage the team. You want to concentrate, focus on the team and it does become tiresome.

'You become a politician. You become constantly talking about side issues rather than issues you want to talk about.

'I had to work hard to keep an equilibrium about the place. The way things were, it was tough. But that's my job.

'During my time there, there was so many side issues we had to deal with that at times the football came second.

'We were so close to not making a certain deadline prior to the first game of the season at Crawley. We had to register all our players for the first game of the season and there were so many non-certainties about the situation.

'There were a lot of issues.'

Asked if the situation ever affected his relationship with the club's board, he said: 'It's not something I really want to discuss. But within the club, I felt I was the one who had to make all the big decisions.

'I don't want to go into my relationship with the others.

'I carried out many aspects of the job in what I would consider to be remarkable circumstances.

'Not just the moving of the stadium, the two ten-point deductions, but when you consider at the same time as that I'm having to drastically reduce wage levels, play young players – it's a mammoth task.

'I loved my time there, so many challenges, but I loved it. I think it's a club with such great potential.'

It was, of course, impossible for the players to be completely shielded from the situation.

Fans' favourite Carl Baker was the club captain during this dark time, and he said uncertainty circled the dressing room long before the move to Northampton was finally announced.

The midfielder told me: 'It was obviously a really difficult time.

'When they were having trouble financially, there were rumours we were going to have to leave and that they couldn't afford to pay the wages.

'It wasn't just about moving out of the Ricoh, there were loads of things that were going on at the time.

'Players didn't know if they were going to be getting their wages or what stadium they were going to be playing football at.

'From the players' point of view, it was very worrying times – one, you don't know if you're going to get paid, and two, you don't know if you're going to have a contract or where you are going to be playing your football.

'We were often finding out a lot of stuff through the paper and media. Nobody ever sat us down to tell us we were going to be moving away or any of the difficulties that the club were involved in.

'As a player, it was quite frightening because we didn't actually know what was going on.'

He added: 'Unfortunately, the talk in the dressing room, that was what the majority of it was all about, which is the way it is going to be when lads are worried about contracts and where they're going to be playing their football.

'The majority of the senior lads, and the younger lads, were talking about the situation off the field more than the situation on the field.

'As club captain and one of the senior players there at the time, the lads were always asking me did I have any extra information.

'But as club captain, nobody ever pulled me aside and told me anything the others didn't know.

'I had no extra information so we were all a left a bit out of the loop about what was going to happen with ourselves and the club. It was difficult.'

Asked if he thought the off-the-field shenanigans ever affected the players' on-field performances, he said: 'I think it definitely did affect the lads mentally.

'I don't know if it necessarily affected the performances because, as professional football players, when you put that shirt on, whether you go and play at the Ricoh, Wembley or on a Sunday league pitch, it doesn't matter where you play your football.

'I don't think the lads had any excuse for how they performed. I still think every single player will have performed to the maximum and give their all for the shirt and themselves.

'I don't think it affected performances, but it definitely affected the team spirit and bond.

'You look at the Leicester City team that won the Premier League and I think the main reason they won that league is the closeness amongst the lads and the togetherness of the squad.

'We didn't really have that because some of the lads didn't want to be there because they didn't know the future of the club, the direction the club was going in and their heads were turned elsewhere.

'They still performed to the maximum ability going on the pitch but certainly in the dressing room, it wasn't as close as what you would have liked.

'It did upset the lads in that sense.'

Baker also subscribed to the theory that the time at Northampton had a positive impact on some of the younger players in terms of allowing them to develop in a lower-pressure environment.

He said: 'It probably did help some of the players playing at Sixfields. If you actually look at the performances and some of the results in the games we played there, I think during my time at the club it was the best we played.

'Results-wise, we were doing well when we first went there.

'The Ricoh with the Coventry fans is a really tough place to play. As well as the expectation and the demands they put on the players, with the club having been successful in the past they want it to be back there and rightly so.

'The demands they put on the players is massive. They're playing for a club where the fans demand so much from the players.

'When things aren't going their way, it can be a really difficult crowd to play in front of and a really difficult stadium to play in.

'On the flip side of that, it can also be the best stadium and the best fans to play in front of. If you are winning and performing well, they will back you to the hilt and you feel that when you're on the pitch.

'But on the other side, if you're not performing well and results aren't going your way – and we did have a young squad at the time – then the Ricoh is a really difficult place to play.

'I certainly agree that playing at Sixfields will have helped the younger lads. Maybe it took a lot of pressure off them. There weren't as many fans there, and it would have helped them perform, and they would have felt a bit more confident playing there.'

But Baker said any positives for the younger players were far outweighed by the negatives of playing at Sixfields.

He said: 'One hundred per cent, the situation made players want to leave and put people off joining.

'For myself personally, I never, ever wanted to leave Coventry. But one of the reasons I signed at Coventry was because of the Ricoh.

'I remember going to speak to a couple of clubs, including Coventry, when I was leaving Stockport and one of the main factors of me wanting to sign for Coventry was the stadium and the training facilities.

'If that affected my decision, then I'm sure for players who are coming to the club the stadium is a big attraction for getting players into the club.

'We didn't have that attraction because we wasn't playing there. It's not as glamorous signing for Coventry playing at Sixfields as signing for Coventry playing at the Ricoh, unfortunately.

'There would have been a lot of players who wanted to leave at the time and maybe players the club were trying to get in who wouldn't have fancied it as much as if we were playing at the Ricoh.'

Asked if playing at Sixfields was a factor in top scorer Leon Clarke leaving the club during the 2013/14 season, he said: 'Possibly, you would have to ask Leon. He was obviously enjoying his football and scoring goals and performing well.

'It can't have been anything to do with on the pitch that he was upset with.

'The fact is there would have been a financial attraction and fees and the chance to play in front of a big crowd.

'Every player wants to play in front of big crowds in big stadiums and at the highest level they can.

'I don't know if Coventry were still at the Ricoh and getting good attendances, maybe it would have been easier to keep Leon.

'But saying that, if you look at Leon's record and how many clubs he's had, he's not the type of lad who stays at one club and he moves about quite a lot.

'It wouldn't surprise me if Sixfields would have meant keeping hold of players was more difficult.

'Players want to play in front of big crowds, and it wasn't like that at Sixfields really.'

Baker said he found it hard to contain his own feelings about the move.

He said: 'I was gutted, absolutely gutted. At first, I didn't believe it when the rumours were going about.

'I thought it was a load of dancing, that it was never going to happen.

'The first time I was actually driving there for a home game was the first time I actually thought "oh my god, this has gone through" and it was going to happen.

'As a player, I was gutted. I loved playing at the Ricoh and in front of the Coventry fans.

'Going to a stadium that was empty, with fans having to sit up on a hill to watch the game, and the facilities and the playing surface we had at the Ricoh wasn't there at Sixfields.

'Travelling-wise, people move to the area to be closer to home games.

'Sitting in your car and having to drive almost an hour to get to a home game is not ideal.

'It's one of those things that is out of the players' hands. You don't have a choice, you just do what you're told basically and try and perform your best, no matter where you are playing.

'Deep down inside it was really difficult, from a player's point of view, to accept.'

He added: 'The players paid a lot of attention to what was going on. It was all we talked about in the dressing room.

'For me personally, I was doing a lot of interviews at the time as the club captain. I remember saying to a reporter "I hope this interview is going to be about football" because I must have done ten or 15 interviews and I didn't get asked a single question about football.

'It was all to do with the Ricoh and Sixfields and all the problems off the field.

'I can't remember being asked about the opposition team or any of our players or the league or anything like that.

'It did become a bit tiresome speaking about that all the time.

'From the players' point of view you tried to turn a blind eye to it, but it was almost impossible to do that.

'Every newspaper article written, every time we put Sky Sports News on or went on the BBC website or whatever, it was always there.

'We did try to get our heads down and concentrate on football, but it was really difficult to do that because it was always in your face.'

Asked how much the match day experience changed for the players, he said: 'There was nothing major that changed but the travelling, and that wasn't ideal. The food preparation had to change and stuff.

'For me, I have got OCD about preparation on a match day and the day before a match day. I like to do everything like clockwork – I eat the same food at the same time and travel the same way to the stadium.

'For me personally, it was difficult because I couldn't be eating my beans on toast while driving to Sixfields.

'So I'd have to eat earlier or take food with me to go. Sometimes we'd go into the training ground and eat pre-match there before travelling on to Sixfields.

'It felt like it was an away game every week. I'm not saying there's anything wrong with that, because you still prepare properly for an away game, but it would have been nice to have some home games in front of your home fans.

'There were times as Sixfields where the away fans outnumbered our home fans. It's difficult enough playing away at the best of times, so to have all your home games feeling like they're away from home, you can imagine what that was like.

'Just the fact you're playing at home probably gets you ten to 12 points a season. When the fans get behind you and make it a difficult place to go and teams have to travel to you, it gets you points throughout the season.

'We didn't have that.'

At times, the supporters on the hill and those who boycotted the games probably felt as if they were fighting a losing battle. But Baker said the players always respected what they were doing and felt for them.

He said: 'We did notice the fans on the hill because at times there were more fans up there than there were in the stadium.

'Obviously it was the first thing you could see. You could see the hill clearly from the stadium, you could see all the banners and hear all the songs whilst you were playing.

'It was impossible to avoid it. All that was in the media all the time, so it was always in your face.

'We understood why the fans didn't go. Obviously we appreciated the fans who did go and supported us and the team and went into the stadium.

'I know it was a really difficult decision.

'I know one family, a married couple who are good friends of mine; they've been Coventry fans their whole life for 30-odd years and they were divided over it.

'The husband was going into the stadium and the wife was going up on the hill. For me, that was crazy and it just shows how passionate some people were.

'This was a husband and wife who had been going to games together for over 30 years and they didn't sit together while they were at Sixfields.

'So that, for me, showed how much it hurt the fans and how much it meant to them.

'We appreciated the fans who did go in, but we also understood the fans who didn't.'

Asked about his overriding feelings over the situation retrospectively, he said: 'I feel a little bit sad when I look back on it, that's probably the best way to describe it.

'I missed a full season playing at the Ricoh in front of the fans. Your football career is only very short. I would have loved to have spent that year playing at the Ricoh. But it wasn't to be.

'I would like to think it could have been avoided. We didn't find out too much inside information.

'Everything can be avoided. The impression we had was that it was a clash of heads at the top between Sisu and the council and the club and ACL.

'It sounded like they were all being childish, threw their teddies out the pram and weren't even willing to negotiate or sit down and come up with a solution.

'I always felt it was going to get sorted. I could never imagine Coventry City not playing at the Ricoh or not playing at home. In my opinion, the club was too big for that and too well supported for that. It's crazy that it actually got to the stage where it did happen.

'But I would like to think it could have been resolved. If people look back now, I'm sure they will admit that they've made mistakes and I'm sure they wish they had maybe sat around a table and bashed something out.

'I don't think anyone won at the end of it. Nobody came out of it on top and nobody was happy about the whole situation of ending up at Sixfields.'

For Sky Blues defender Jordan Clarke, the move to Sixfields had a bigger impact than it did for the vast majority of the club's senior players. Clarke is a Coventry kid, with a long list of family members who are dedicated club supporters.

He revealed the move even meant his mum felt she couldn't come and watch her own son play for his home-town club.

He said: 'My family are all Coventry City fans. My dad came to every game but my mum didn't go. She used to go to the Ricoh but she wouldn't go to Northampton.

'It was a bit of a protest and a bit because it was so far away. She thought, "they're taking the p***"

'She thought, "I've got to travel god knows how long to see my son play for a professional side which has been forced out of its home ground."

'At times, we were told by the club not to talk about the situation too much to family members and so on. But at times, I don't think certain stuff got revealed to us anyway.'

Asked when he had first heard that the club might have to leave Coventry, he said: 'It was around about the time everybody else started to hear about it, but obviously we found out a little bit before the public through in-house stuff.

'The players initially were more worried about means of getting to each game. The players who lived in Coventry had an easy task in getting to the Ricoh, but driving to Sixfields we didn't know if travel would be sorted out or whatnot.

'The players were frustrated, I was. We were going from the Ricoh, which was a great stadium with good facilities and an all round feel-good home ground, to a foreign ground we knew nothing about.

'The stadium obviously wasn't up to the same level as the Ricoh, but once we got over that I think everything about the move was pretty seamless.'

Clarke said he tried to focus on the football rather than the off-field distractions.

He said: 'None of us really understood the financial side of things or the decisions above us.

'We had heard from staff around the place and reading the media coverage, but other than that we didn't really pay much attention.

'Our job was to concentrate on the football. At the time, we didn't really have too much of an idea as to why we were doing it. Most of the players at the time were against it.

'The first game felt like a reserve game, an under-21s type game. It's an away ground to us and a ground in a league below.

'After that it was just a case of, "we're still playing the same teams and we have a job to do".'

The versatile defender said he also believed that young players had benefited from the time at Sixfields, despite the obvious disruption it caused in other areas of the club.

He said: 'I believe playing at Sixfields was a help to all the players because playing at the Ricoh there's a really big pitch and the crowd is quite far away from you.

'Because the Ricoh is so big a ground and we don't fill it, you could hear pretty much everything and for me, personally, after a while I preferred to play at Northampton.

'We just got used to it and it felt like a little bit of pressure was off, to be honest.'

He added: 'Internally and in the changing rooms, everything seemed fine. It was just a case of we are playing games somewhere else.

'I can't remember anyone saying they wanted to leave because we are changing grounds. At the time, we were still at the same level. But I don't know if it put anyone off joining.'

Clarke also said the players backed those who stayed away from games or protested and hit out at those responsible for taking the club out of Coventry.

He said: 'We noticed the protests on the hill every game. I certainly did, anyway.

'Before the start of each game, we would turn around and see them all up there. I was thinking they've probably got the best seats!

'But we've seen them all the time and they always seemed to be in good spirits. It was all for a good cause in getting us back to the Ricoh.

'We were pleased with it.'

He added: 'I think the whole situation could have been avoided. I don't know what the hierarchy at the club, and the people who owned the club, what their end goal is or was.

'For me, knowing what I did know, it was definitely avoidable and I think it was a bit petty, to be honest.

'It should never have happened.'

Chapter 13

#BringCityHome

WHILE Coventry's season ticked along 35 miles away in Northampton, there was also plenty of manoeuvring behind the scenes.

During autumn 2013 there were open letters, private letters, private meetings, public statements and much more between the owners of Coventry City FC and council officials. Council officials were apparently attempting to persuade Sisu to allow the club to return to the Ricoh Arena, but the owners appeared to be adamant that the club could never return as tenants. Furthermore, there now appeared to be a suggestion that only the unencumbered freehold sale of the Ricoh Arena would pave the way for the Sky Blues' return to Coventry. This was a step up from previous talks over merely securing a stake in the Ricoh Arena operating company. Now they wanted the bricks, mortar and land of the arena, which had cost £113m to build.

This was an apparently extreme bargaining position from which Sisu chief Joy Seppala insisted she would not move, and that the club would rather push ahead with its plans for a new stadium than return on a rental basis.

In a rare media interview, Ms Seppala explained her stance to the *Coventry Telegraph*.

She said: 'It's up to them [the council] to decide what their best offer looks like.

'The club needs 100 per cent ownership of the freehold of the Ricoh. If you look back at the history of the club, you can see why this is important.

'I don't posture. I always tell people what it is I need. I don't go for wasting time in negotiations.

'There is no way we would go back to a rental deal. As I have said to the Football League when they asked recently if we would do a temporary arrangement, it would be irrational to return on an interim basis where I have any exposure to Coventry City Council whatsoever.

'The league chairman Greg Clarke has said it is not for the league to dictate what stadium a club plays in, or on what terms.

'Realistically, this council don't think they can work with me. I know I cannot work with them. It doesn't mean I can't negotiate a deal. But I am not going to risk my investors' money by exposing us to the potential of having a repeat of what happened over the last year.

'Would I be open to listening to what they have to say? I would. That is strictly for the fans. I feel empathy for the fans' position. It is not fair what's being done to them. They haven't deserved what's happened to the club over the last 12 months.

'But everything we've done is to implement a long-term strategy that will see the viability of this club for the long term.

'From the moment a decision was made for a joint venture with the council for the Ricoh Arena [in 2003], the club lost control.

'It would be crazy from a business perspective to go back to the Ricoh without full control. All the money that's been put into this club would be put at risk again.

'When the former owners of the club sold the 50 per cent share to Higgs [Alan Edward Higgs Charity], I do not believe they thought they were giving away match day revenues. They thought they had sold the equity stake in the stadium, not the revenues.'

Despite Joy Seppala's comments here, you may remember in Chapter One that Coventry City Council's John McGuigan and long-term club board member Geoffrey Robinson seemed to indicate the club knew exactly what they were getting into during the sale of the stake in ACL –and had been specifically warned about the revenue issue. The facts seem to suggest the club simply didn't have an alternative at the point they sold their share in ACL if the Ricoh Arena project was to be delivered and if the club were going to avoid administration in 2003.

There was obvious anger and frustration among supporters that their club had been moved out of their home city and that a compromise couldn't be reached at the Ricoh Arena, but Joy Seppala insisted that the owners had acted in the best interests of the football club.

The 'devout Christian' said she had received hate mail, including e-mails containing words such as 'die' and 'bitch'. Despite the abuse, she said she had taken time to respond to more constructive e-mails from fans.

She said: 'Would I have preferred to stay at the Ricoh? Of course. Would I have preferred to reach a deal with the council? Of course. That's why we agreed to the heads of terms [for the Higgs share last year]. But for whatever reason, they patently refused to authorise that purchase.

'We have made decisions which we believe are emphatically the right decisions and we're in the right place. We're taking the club in the right direction, bar the emotional angst it's given to fans. Emotions are not lost on us. I feel very bad. Football is like a religion.

'The long-term viability of the club depends on us doing this. If the status quo continued, Coventry City would not be here in a year or two.'

But Joy Seppala's comments in the press appeared to do little to smooth relations with the council. Coventry City Council leader Ann Lucas reacted by issuing a public statement which said the council was willing to discuss stadium ownership with Sisu but that 'time was running out'.

She said: 'All options are available for discussion. I am prepared to discuss, subject to contract, and without prejudice to the on-going court case, the issue of stadium ownership with Joy Seppala, just as I have been prepared to discuss stadium ownership with other interested third parties in the past.

'If this matter cannot be resolved by the turn of the year, then I and all of my colleagues on the Labour group on Coventry City Council will look to put in place a process which ensures the best possible deal for the people of Coventry in relation to the Ricoh Arena.

"So for one last time, I say, quite clearly, that I am prepared to meet with Joy Seppala and to have a discussion with her without prejudice and subject to contract in relation to all and any issues in relation to the Ricoh Arena, the land around it, and Coventry City Football Club.'

The significance of this statement was probably missed at the time, including by the media. The 'other interested parties' line seemed like nothing more than posturing at the time. Now, of course, we know there was one extremely interested party – Wasps Rugby Football Club.

But, at the time, all the public signs seemed to suggest ACL was desperately scratching around for ways to recover the £1.3m it had lost in revenue following the termination of Coventry City's licence to use the stadium.

During an interview with newly appointed ACL chairman Chris Robinson shortly after these public statements, it was revealed the stadium could even look to play host to Coventry Speedway.

Aside from the odd charity football match, the stadium bowl's major event of summer 2014 was a streaking contest organised by a microwaveable burger firm and judged by members of the cast from *The Only Way is Essex*. Really, I'm not joking – this actually happened.

The stadium was even struggling to attract the major music gigs it had staged in the past, and the company was clearly struggling as staff numbers shrank.

ACL director Peter Knatchbull-Hugessen even told me the firm had looked at playing host to monster trucks to fill the void left by the Coventry City.

Non-executive director Mark Labovitch was always very keen to emphasise how badly the Ricoh business was performing during this period. He pointed towards big payments from the casino operators and the naming rights sponsors in the early days, which had been averaged out over proceeding years to make the numbers in the accounts look more promising.

He was, of course, right.

During this period, I asked Mr Labovitch directly if the club wanted ACL to fold.

He said: 'It's none of our business, we want to run a football club.

'It would help it they were not there.'

It's apparent now that a waiting game was being played to see who could hold out the longest: ACL on reduced stadium revenues or the club on reduced income and falling attendances? Council officials continued to talk up ACL's business performance and club bosses their own and so the wait went on as stadium discussions fell away yet again.

In December 2013, the club was offered a deal by ACL which would have apparently seen it return to the Ricoh Arena rent free until the end of the season – and £100,000 for each of the next two seasons if they remained in League One.

But the club complained the proposal failed to offer the loss-making club any vital stadium revenues, and would still have seen them paying other match day costs totalling £320,000 a year.

Speaking to the *Coventry Telegraph* at the time, Mark Labovitch said: 'We have made it clear that no club can have a viable financial future unless it owns its own stadium.

'There is no prospect of us returning to the former landlord/tenant relationship with ACL, a company which bled the club dry for many years over two generations of owners, and wilfully sought to damage the club with actions which led to needless points deductions over the last two seasons.

'Such inexplicable actions have severely damaged our promotion chances. It is a credit to Steven Pressley and the players that so much of the damage caused by ACL has been made good.

'Joy's door is open to Ann for further discussions. But we would have to be clear this time that it would be a discussion about stadium ownership.

'In the absence of a clear commitment to discuss ownership, we are pressing ahead with the plans for our new stadium on the outskirts of Coventry.'

An ACL spokesman responded: 'A further attempt to bring the Sky Blues home to Coventry was made recently by Arena Coventry Limited.

'A rent-free offer, with the club only paying match day costs, was made via the Football League, who offered to act as brokers to a deal.

'The offer was made on the basis that the club could come back to Coventry immediately and then negotiations of a more permanent settlement could begin again in earnest. At present, no formal response has been received.

'ACL would, of course, welcome the Sky Blues back to their home stadium and are available to do so at short notice. We have an open-door policy on discussions to achieve this and will make every effort to do so if called upon.'

In January 2014, the Sky Blue Army vented their frustration in high-profile fashion.

Supporters who travelled to The Emirates for Coventry City's FA Cup fourth-round clash with Premier League Arsenal drew national attention to the club's plight with a powerful visual protest.

Led by the *Keep Cov in Cov* protest group, fans held signs with the word 'why' aloft on 35 minutes – symbolising the distance the club had been moved from the Ricoh Arena to play 'home' matches.

While the team might not have made much of an impact, eventually succumbing to a 4-0 defeat, the fans certainly did. Their pain and anguish was broadcast into the living rooms of fellow football supporters across the country.

The situation at Coventry City finally boiled over in March 2014, when Coventry City chief executive Tim Fisher was attacked by fans in a London pub after a match.

About 20 supporters were said to have been involved in the incident, which occurred as Mr Fisher went to use the bar's toilet. He was apparently pelted with drinks and chairs as he waited for a train following the team's 3-1 defeat away at Brentford.

The attack was roundly condemned by the vast majority of supporters and it later emerged that other fans had attempted to intervene.

Mr Fisher escaped serious injury and the matter was not reported to police.

One supporter who witnessed the incident was Juggy Chima.

He said Mr Fisher had offered to buy supporters a drink before the trouble flared up.

He added: 'There must have been about 25 or 20 City fans in there, some we see quite often and a few that we had never seen before.

'Everyone is having a drink and then suddenly Tim Fisher walks in and went the toilet. Where the toilets were, you had to go right through the pub to get to the toilets.

'At first, when he went in, sort of a buzz went up "that's Tim Fisher."'

He added: 'Obviously people have had a drink. Where he came out of the toilets, there was a bit of singing going on, 'we want Sisu out' and all that.

'The guy had actually given somebody some money to say get everybody a drink.

'There was a split. Some people were singing and some people were fine saying, 'the guy has just come in to use the toilet, just let him get on with it.'

'As he was leaving, the chants went up and there were one or two trying to stop him from leaving the pub and then one or two were trying to push them out the way, just saying 'let the guy go.'

'There was no actual glasses or bottles thrown, but somebody threw some beer on him. And then there was a bit of a surge from two or three people and some stools went flying. He was jostled and he was manhandled, there's no two ways about that.'

He added: 'When he got outside, Steve Waggott was waiting and the two of them made a sharp exit because, obviously, they don't know how the situation is going to pan out – because everybody started to come out.

'People were saying "go" because there had been a lot of beer drunk. This situation could have ended with someone getting a smack and then that's really going to take it to another level.

'The general consensus was that this is what happens when fans aren't given their voice.'

Emotions surrounding the club were obviously running high and the violence was not the ideal preparation as the club's owners prepared for a court battle with the Higgs Charity a few weeks later.

It was at this court hearing I had my first face-to-face encounter with Mr Fisher since I had joined the *Coventry Telegraph*. Whether he was unhappy with my report of the pub attack a week earlier, I'm not sure. But it's fair to say he didn't greet me in an overly friendly manner.

Standing in the lobby of Birmingham High Court, he towered over me, pointed his finger in my face and said: 'You know what I think of you.'

My reply of 'Actually Tim, I don't, why don't you tell me?' probably didn't help in hindsight – but that's what happened.

In fairness to Mr Fisher, it was evidently an extremely stressful time, and I'm not one to hold a grudge. There was also a half apology from him the following day in court, when we had a lengthy chat during a lunchtime break in which he issued some handy career advice.

But I think it's fair to say I'm still not his preferred contact in the press.

As we know, the Higgs hearing ended in a 0-0 draw as the charity's claim and Sisu's counter-claim were both thrown out.

But it wasn't our last trip to court that year. In June 2014, we were back for the long-awaited judicial review into Coventry City Council's £14.4m bail-out of Ricoh Arena firm ACL.

There was more pettiness during this hearing and I saw ACL director Peter Knatchbull-Hugessen waving and blowing kisses to Mr Fisher from the opposite side of the courtroom at one point. Another example of the type of unnecessary antagonistic behaviour that had no doubt been displayed by all sides from time to time and led to the disgraceful situation of Coventry City being moved out of their home city.

As the judicial review came to a close, Mark Labovitch said and did some bizarre things which I believe ultimately led to his demise and departure from club's board.

On the final day of the hearing, viewed by those at Sisu as arguably one of the most important days in the club's history, Mr Labovitch sent his first-ever tweet from the courtroom – a comment taking the mickey out of my haircut.

Now, admittedly, I have a history of bad haircuts. But this was hardly seen as the time or the place to be making jokes by others within the club's hierarchy – or the fans.

But what really did it for Mark Labovitch, in my opinion, was the interview he gave to then sports editor Keith Perry and I on the court steps.

He said: 'This is a side show that has nothing to do with the football club.

'The city has a problem. The club isn't playing in the city. There's a problem that needs to be solved and this is not part of that solution. Is it going to be easier to get around the table now? I really don't know. I hope so.'

The suggestion that the expensive judicial review process was nothing more than 'a side show' clearly did not sit well with the club's owners or others on the Coventry board. And there was no room for any suggestion he had been misquoted this time as two journalists had heard him use these words.

Three months later, Mark Labovitch stepped down from the board as part of a reshuffle which also saw Tim Fisher move to the role of chairman and Steve Waggott take over as chief executive.

The judicial review judgement has already been comprehensively covered in this book, so I won't waste too much time explaining what happened after the hearing here. Suffice to say the council successfully defended the legal challenge and Sisu continues to appeal that decision through the courts at the time of writing.

With the court action out of the way for the time being, focused shifted back on to Coventry City FC and how the club could be returned to its home city.

Several protest groups had emerged during the dispute, including the anti-council *Get Cov Back to the Ricoh* group. A damp squib of a protest outside the council's Earl Street base attracted a handful of supporters as the group announced it would be fielding a candidate in the forthcoming local elections against council leader Ann Lucas.

But former councillor Brian Patton suffered a crushing defeat as he attracted just 235 votes – finishing fifth out of the six candidates in the ward and 1,727 votes behind councillor Lucas.

Other fans continued to do what they could to force a return, and at the start of July 2014 a campaign group called

Keep Cov in Cov, led by supporter Michael Orton, tabled an offer to pay the club's rent at the Ricoh Arena for three years. The group had attracted support from local businessmen – including former vice-chairman Gary Hoffman – and said it would only seek to be reimbursed once attendances at the Ricoh Arena topped 5,000.

But Tim Fisher rejected the suggestion out of hand.

He said: 'I'm sure Michael Orton's motivations are well meaning but these discussions have never been about rent.

'The discussion is around revenues. This club needs to control and manage its match day revenues. That is not in his gift.

'If there were an interim deal on the table, do you not think we would pay the rent?

'We don't need anybody to pay the rent.

'We are fully aware of the local businessman behind this. He is part of the problem, not the solution.'

The club had just spent an entire season at an alien ground and the thought of the club's fans having to face another season watching their club die a slow and painful death from afar was harrowing.

At this time I knew there was an important meeting coming up, a chance to apply some pressure on all the parties involved and move closer to finally ending this Sixfields nightmare.

In August 2014 ACL, Coventry Council, Higgs Charity and club officials would get together at the Football League's headquarters in London.

The summit was to discuss the settlement of a £470,000 bill the club had to pay ACL as a result of the administration of CCFC Ltd.

Sisu appeared to be digging their heels in over paying the bill and it was a clear barrier to any possible return to the Ricoh Arena.

They had argued that £300,000 ACL had received from former chairman Geoffrey Robinson and Mike McGinnity should be deducted from the bill. The pair had acted as rent guarantors for CCFC and had been successfully pursed for £150,000 each as the rent row escalated.

Geoffrey Robinson said he believed the guarantees should have disappeared with the sale to Sisu in 2007.

He told me: 'It should have been extinguished at the time we did the sale to Sisu.

'We both thought it was, it was a failure on our part – and of our lawyers – to ensure that it was terminated. It was an oversight.

'But they didn't have any hesitation in coming after us, despite everything we'd lost. Mike had lost a million or two.

'It was legal, but did it reflect the spirit of the whole thing? No, it was very mean.

'We just paid up. Mike said "I can't go through a court case, Geoffrey, settle" – so I settled. He and I have remained firm friends right through to the end.'

Speaking to me at the time about being forced to hand over the money, the late Mr McGinnity said: 'I'm absolutely disgusted. To say I'm disappointed in the current situation at the club is an understatement.

'We hoped it would go from strength to strength but that wasn't the case.

'At the time, we thought the Sisu takeover was right. It's a disgrace. I hate to think what they are losing now.

'What's the point in building another stadium when they have a perfectly good one where serious adults could sit down and work something out?

'Sir Derek Higgs must be turning in his grave. None of this would have happened if he'd still been alive, I'm certain of that.

'I'm absolutely fed up to the back teeth of it and I feel extremely sorry for the fans.'

He added: 'Would I do anything differently? Most certainly; I wouldn't get involved.

'It has cost me a lot of money and Geoffrey ten times as much.'

With the Football League meeting approaching, I emphasised my feelings to the then-editor Alun Thorne and sports editor Keith Perry that this was the time to strike if we wanted to have a real impact on the situation. But we couldn't do it alone.

Any campaign would have to be fan-led, with the *Coventry Telegraph* providing the platform and support necessary to make sure the message reached those who needed to hear it.

The idea of a campaign had already been suggested by Keith and Alun came up with the name - #BringCityHome.

In July 2014, the *Coventry Telegraph* launched the campaign, and I took the lead on the editorial side.

The paper encouraged fans to take pictures with the #BringCityHome slogan and a giant billboard was sent to the headquarters of all the key players – including the London offices of Sisu and the Football League as well as Coventry Council House and the Ricoh Arena.

The message was simple 'Enough is enough. The time has long since passed for Coventry City to come home.'

Another protest march was organised by the Sky Blue Trust and attracted more fans than the first, underlining that – while their club might have gone away – the Sky Blue Army's passion for their club never left.

But the true pressure to resolve the situation would come from the political arena.

Every MP in Coventry and Warwickshire pledged their support to our campaign, along with celebrities from the world of sport and television.

Crucially, I had previously established contact with Conservative MP Damian Collins, who was leading the calls for the reformation of football.

He had previously been scathing in his criticism of Sisu and the Football League.

In March 2014, he told me: 'The owners of Coventry City have run the club into the ground. It is an absolute disgrace what they have done there and it should not be allowed to happen again.'

He added: 'We have to stop private individuals running clubs into the ground.

'Coventry City is probably the most stark example in the country of just how bad the situation is at the moment.'

'At Coventry City, we don't even know who owns the club. Anyone who owns any stake in the club has to be published.

'I don't think it's right that fans don't who the owners of their club are. There are many reasons why fans would want to know that.

'We want to know where they have come from and what their motivation is.'

'The reason Coventry have left is because of the financial situation the club has got itself into.

'It should be a matter for the FA to determine whether a club should be able to move away. A club and its ground should be locked together.

'It should not be allowed to happen where we have a situation like Coventry's where the team plays miles away from their home city.'

Knowing about Mr Collins' passion for reformation, I saw an opportunity to apply pressure on the Football League. If the club's owners did not pay the £470,000 they had been ordered to through the administration procedure, it would call into question the controversial 'football creditors rule' – which allows other members of the football family to be paid ahead of any other creditors when a club becomes insolvent.

Mr Collins was campaigning to scrap this rule already, as were HMRC. I flagged up the situation at the club to both Mr Collins and HMRC shortly before the crucial meeting to see what the impact would be if a resolution was not found.

Mr Collins said: 'This could be a prime example of the failure of the football creditors rule and a prompt for action.

'I am monitoring the situation. It will be a concern if the stadium doesn't get that money and the club walks away.

'I think the Football League has to order the club to pay the full amount. It is money the club fairly owes. They entered into the agreement and they should honour it.

'There is no justification for the football creditors rule. It is massively unfair on other creditors and the community and it encourages irresponsible financial behaviour.'

He added: 'Coventry is the worst example in football at the moment of the problems clubs can get into with poor ownership and the need for the FA and the Football League to intervene.

'If governing bodies won't act, they need to be forced to through legislation.

'This situation is appalling. It underlines that Sisu should never have been allowed to take over the club and run it the way they have done.

'They are an example of how a bad owner can destroy a football club and it should never be able to happen again.

'The situation at Coventry underlined the importance and the need for legislation. The problem hasn't gone away and they need to act.'

A spokesman for HMRC said: 'Our view remains that the football creditor rule is unfair to all other unsecured creditors who are forced to make do with much smaller returns – if anything – on monies owed to them by football clubs which enter administration.'

Just to be sure Football League officials were aware the football creditors rule was potentially under threat, I travelled to London to hand-deliver copies of the *Coventry Telegraph* on the day of the crucial meeting. They were very special editions which also featured the faces of scores of Coventry City fans holding placards emblazoned with the #BringCityHome slogan

The comments from the Conservative MP seemingly focused minds at the Football League. We soon learnt that the required payment had been made by the club's owners and another major hurdle to the club's return had been removed.

Coventry North East MP Bob Ainsworth said he had little doubt that the comments from Mr Collins had played an important role in removing the roadblock to peace talks.

He said: 'When Damian Collins became involved, and with him being a Tory and in power, that had a huge impact.

'When he started talking about the potential for the football creditors' rule to be scrapped, we thought that was the best way into the Football League.

'I had raised it with ministers, and they said it changed the game.

'Why in hell has football got this special arrangement that no other area of business enjoys?

'Jeremy Wright was also quite helpful. He wrote letters and spoke to colleagues in government.

'Hugh Robertson, who was minister for sport at the time, was also very helpful.'

ACL board director Peter Knatchbull-Hugessen agreed that the political pressure was the biggest factor in getting the Football League to act.

He told me: 'The Football League's priority seemed to be protecting its member and not being seen by other members to be causing a problem for a member.

'The Football League was undoubtedly heavily influenced by the political pressure and the suggestion that the football creditors rule could be lost if this situation wasn't resolved satisfactorily.

'The deal on the table at that Football League meeting had to be taken.

'The political pressure was there because of the campaigns and the marches, and because of the work of people like Bob Ainsworth and Damian Collins, who were extremely helpful. It helps to have that noise.

'The pressure from the public couldn't really influence the decisions we made as directors because our responsibilities were fixed. But did it make people work longer hours to find a solution? Absolutely.'

Finally, we seemed to be making progress. But the club wasn't back yet.

Secretly, and away from the glare of the public, meetings were taking place between all of the key parties.

In mid-August 2014, I had learned from my sources that a deal had been agreed for the club to return to the Ricoh Arena. Frustratingly, I had to sit on this story for almost a week at the request of the parties involved. Of course, we obliged. If the deal was going to collapse at this late stage, it wasn't going to be because of the *Coventry Telegraph*.

On 21 August, at 1pm, we broke the news. I had never been more excited about breaking a story in my life. Initially, some people refused to believe it, which was understandable bearing in mind the huge setbacks supporters had faced over the years.

But as the official statements started to drip out over the next few hours, the city rejoiced. Coventry City were coming home.

But how had they got there? There were many interesting claims at the time, but the truth of the matter emerged during my research for this book.

My favourite story was probably when Coventry Cathedral attempted to suggest they had been responsible for the club's return.

Reverend John Witcombe, the Dean of Coventry, suggested he had set the ball rolling by travelling to London to meet Sisu boss Joy Seppala. Frankly, the idea that this had unlocked the situation was nonsense – but the opportunity to use the headline 'Divine intervention' was perhaps too good an opportunity to pass up.

Two people who undoubtedly played a key role were ACL chairman Chris Robinson and the club's chief executive Steve Waggott.

The pair were relatively new faces in the context of the long-running battle and were perhaps able to bring fresh perspective as they negotiated for a week behind the scenes.

Chris Robinson said: 'A fresh perspective can only help. The negotiations were conducted in great spirit between Steve Waggott and I.

'I think there will always be moments when you have doubts. You always have those thoughts, but ultimately we knew we could get there.

'Negotiations can always be tough. But when both people want to achieve success, that makes a huge difference.'

Steve Waggott even revealed, during the course of negotiations, he went 48 hours without sleep – such was the appetite to ensure the club returned to Coventry.

He said: 'Chris Robinson and I started with no hidden agenda but we had lots of disagreements and both had to make concessions before we found a middle point.

'We kept our sights on getting us back to Coventry and I certainly wasn't going to leave the room until a deal was signed. And I'm delighted, not just for the football club but for the city.'

But there was only so much Mr Robinson and Mr Waggott could agree on. Any final decision would ultimately be down to the ACL board and Sisu boss Joy Seppala.

What happened next is somewhat controversial. ACL's board drew up a list of 'red lines' for any deal which would see the club return to the Ricoh Arena. Crucially, the Higgs Charity – as joint stakeholders in ACL – ordered that any deal would only be agreed if all legal action was dropped by Sisu.

Council officials and Chris Robinson later travelled to London without the permission of ACL's board to meet Ms Seppala and negotiate a return to the stadium. But, on arrival, they discovered that the right to continue with legal action was also a red line for Sisu.

It looked as if there would be another stalemate. At this point councillor Phil Townshend, deputy leader of Coventry City Council, stepped in. With leader Ann Lucas out of the country on annual leave, he had been thrust into the hot seat.

In a candid private conversation at the time, the late Cllr Townshend revealed to me that he had threatened to resign from the council if officers didn't agree a deal for a return – and that Sisu must be allowed to continue legal action.

Council officers subsequently rubber-stamped the deal – with no pre-requisite for legal action to be dropped.

But not everyone was entirely happy, and the consequences of that red line being crossed are still being felt today.

Peter Knatchbull-Hugessen, Higgs Charity clerk and then ACL board member, told me: 'The charity had clear red lines. One of those was that legal action must be dropped. No more legal action could be started on anything already open.

'Then the chairman of ACL, Chris Robinson and Chris West from the council [also a director of ACL] went down to London to meet Joy Seppala and Alex Carter-Silk [one of Sisu's legal team] without the ACL board's permission.

'Against the board's approval, and directly against our red lines, they negotiated a return to the Ricoh Arena. People were deliberately excluded from those conversations.

'We could have avoided further legal action and JR1 would have ended.

'But it was excellent that they came back. The club was back where it should be.'

Chapter 14

Sting in the tail

O N 5 September 2014, one of the greatest wrongs in the history of Coventry City – and possibly English football – was righted when the Sky Blues returned to the city which gave the club its name, its history and its passion.

More than 27,000 supporters flocked to the Ricoh Arena to see the Sky Blues take on Gillingham and sneak a 1-0 victory. The short notice of the return had caused obvious ticketing issues, otherwise every seat in the house would have been filled. In the days preceding the game, thousands of fans had queued for hours to get their hands on tickets – but nobody cared about this when the game kicked off. Coventry City were back where they belonged. Coventry City were home.

The importance of Coventry City returning to their home city was summed up by the story of terminally ill Steve Grant.

The 66-year-old, from Ash Green, feared he would never see his beloved Sky Blues play again after being diagnosed with inoperable cancer the previous year.

But, on that night, his dying wish was granted when his team returned to their home city.

He could barely hold back the tears as he explained what the team's return meant to him – and thousands of others.

He said: 'What can you say? I'm speechless. I'm over the moon, it really is fantastic.

'I didn't think I would ever see it. Not many things can brighten your life up when you're in a situation like mine, but this really has.

'I couldn't understand rhyme or reason why we were in Northampton.

'You can't call them Coventry when they are playing in Northampton. I felt we had been robbed.'

It was a day to look forward, rather than back, as differences were set aside and former foes became friendly.

Jacky Isaac, chief executive of Ricoh Arena operators ACL, said: 'It is brilliant, we are absolutely delighted. We are delighted with the atmosphere and the crowd.

'It is fantastic for the fans and it is great that they have come out in such huge numbers to support the Sky Blues.

'All of a sudden it has become very familiar. It's almost like we are back to how we were.'

The message of reconciliation was also pushed by newly appointed Coventry City chief executive Steve Waggott.

He said: 'It feels right that we have reunited the club with Coventry and the Ricoh Arena for all the right positive reasons. It is the first step to moving the club forward.

'To get the response we have had, from the time Chris Robinson [ACL chairman] and I signed the agreement to 28,000 fans turning up, it makes the work of the teams at CCFC and ACL worth it. When we see the people coming in buzzing, it is everything that football should do to unite a community. The partnership we have with ACL, it has been a really positive new start to the relationship, and long may it continue. We are working for the mutual benefits of the club, ACL and the Coventry community.'

The return was obviously a special time for the management team, which had endured huge tests over the previous season. Team manager Steven Pressley admitted the scale of the occasion had overwhelmed him at times and he was even moved to tears.

He told me: 'I was very emotional that night. I actually cried that night because it was so emotional.

'My staff and I had gone through such turmoil, so many challenges and to come back that night and play in front of a crowd of that level, with that support and that passion to watch us as a team was hugely emotional for us. It was a difficult night.'

Although he was delighted to be back in Coventry, Pressley said returning had actually been a disaster from a football perspective. He also emphasised how unprepared the stadium seemed to be for the club's return.

He said: 'It didn't look likely. The truth is in the first season there had been no investment in the Northampton pitch. In the second season, the club made an investment along with Northampton to bring the playing surface up to a better standard.

'It looked very much like we would be at Northampton for another season. Then things moved very quickly.

'In a very short period of time, there had been a complete change and it looked like the club would return.

'The biggest problem we found was that we were a team that really wanted to play and pass and the Ricoh Arena, when we returned – I can't tell you how bad the playing surface was.

'There had been no preparation work. There had been an event held on the pitch just weeks before we were coming to play fixtures there. It had completely ruined the surface.

'It was great to return to the Ricoh, because it was so important to the club and the city, but from a football perspective it was a disaster.

'Because the pitch wasn't being used on a regular basis for top-level football, there was very little in the way of ground staff.

'An incredible thing happened before one game, it may well have been Yeovil at home. We turned up and the grass hadn't been cut.

'My own fitness coach Pete Tierney, along with the one member of ground staff, had to cut the pitch prior to a League One game.

'The pitch dimensions were also something like five metres wider than we had requested. All of these things were far from ideal. I'm not here making excuses, but the fine details are really important and all these things were missing and were not ideal for our preparation.'

He added: 'Another disappointment is that I think the Ricoh is such a big stadium that it's a problem when you don't get such a large crowd.

'What they've done recently in terms of moving the supporters into one area is hugely beneficial. That's vital, they've made a really positive step in that respect.

'I know many supporters have had their seat since the Ricoh opened, but if you're talking about what's best for the football team itself, it's that they create a more intensive atmosphere.'

CCFC Academy graduate Jordan Clarke said the return to play football for his home club in his home city was a day he would never forget – although he also shared the view that, football-wise, it was hugely disruptive.

He told me: 'I remember hearing about the return to the Ricoh [in] the weeks leading up to it.

'At the time, the general feeling was that we are used to Sixfields now and we quite enjoy it there.

'But obviously Coventry was our home town and we were all pleased to go back there.

'It was a case of: we need to adapt to this pitch again, because we used to play on a smaller pitch at Sixfields.

'It was a bit frustrating being moved back and forth but other than that, overall we were pleased to be back.'

He added: 'The pitch at the Ricoh always was not that great. It was generally more sand than grass and during the winter months it was horrendous really – bobbly and just not good.

'It was not the best because we had just got into our rhythm and we were happy playing there, but it's obviously much better to have your home club in your home town.

'It was great for the city and great for the fans to be able to come to the games again because there were a lot boycotting it.

'It was unbelievable. It is the best atmosphere I played in at Coventry City. Having a stadium filled to the brim for a League One game was unbelievable.

'I got a chance to play in that, and I remember when Frank Nouble got the goal, and it was just an amazing feeling because I've never heard the Ricoh that loud before.

'That first game back I didn't feel any pressure at all. It was more of a buzz.

'After that the crowds got lower, but there was still a lot more than Sixfields.

'As long as you try and play your best and perform at the end of the day, the fans will be happy. Pressure is always there in football.

'The only difference was all of our pictures were gone from the tunnel. The changing room was starting to look bare.

'It wasn't the same look and feel as it was before we left. It was more homely before with our badges everywhere, our quotes on the walls, but when we came back it was pretty much stripped of stuff.

'It was a bit frustrating, but it was just material things.'

Carl Baker, who was club captain when we first left the Ricoh Arena, had moved on before the club's return to the stadium. But the midfielder told me he was delighted for the fans.

He said: 'I finished playing my Coventry football at Sixfields.

'Personally, probably in a selfish way, I was a little bit disappointed and gutted that I wasn't going to be able to play there again.

'It would have been nice for me to lead the team out that season at the Ricoh.

'But from the club's point of view, I was pleased as it gives them a better chance of progressing.

'When they went back to the Ricoh, I was absolutely delighted for everyone involved with the club – especially the fans. I knew how much it meant to them and I knew how passionate they were about it.

'When I heard they were going to go back, I was absolutely buzzing that the football was going to be back in the city where it belonged.'

But as fans revelled in the Sky Blues' return to the stadium, in typical fashion, a sting in the tail soon emerged.

The hope was, now that the club had returned, perhaps a deal for stadium ownership might not be too far off.

I had asked deputy council leader Phil Townshend about this possibility at the time and he told me: 'I think we should take one day at a time and not get ahead of ourselves and use this period to rebuild trust.

'All parties concerned need to learn to open the door for one another as opposed to allowing it to slam in other people's faces.

'There's been too much personal criticism in the past. A conciliatory approach is in the best interests of all parties concerned.'

Weeks later, I had a concerned phone call from Cllr Townshend, who sadly passed away in 2015.

Few would question Mr Townshend's loyalty to the council leadership at that time, but he felt it necessary to tip me off about secret talks going on behind the scenes in relation to the Ricoh Arena.

The council was on the verge of agreeing a deal with Premiership rugby club Wasps to secure the local authority's stake in ACL – with a view to immediately taking the charity's share and therefore complete ownership of the Ricoh Arena firm.

I made enquiries, and sources connected to the football club and the charity confirmed they also had knowledge that Wasps were preparing a takeover package. A prospectus was being floated around the financial elite in London, which had alerted Coventry City officials.

Within 24 hours of first hearing of this development, we broke the news exclusively on the *Coventry Telegraph* website. Nobody would go on the record about the story, and there were borderline denials from some involved – but the cat was now out of the bag.

Had the *Coventry Telegraph* not broken this story, there was every chance the deal for Wasps to take over ACL could have taken place almost entirely in private and away from public scrutiny. It's largely thanks to Cllr Townshend's conscience that the public had an opportunity to voice any opposition to the takeover prior to it being completed.

Over the next few weeks, we revealed further details of the bid, including its value.

The rugby club would pay £2.77m for the council's share of the Ricoh Arena firm and the same amount for the Alan Higgs Charity's share. The sale would represent a major loss for the charity, which had initially invested £6.5m to secure the share in 2003.

Wasps would also take on the remainder of ACL's £14.4m loan from the council and the company's lease would be extended from 50 years to 250 years as part of the deal.

The council's share of ACL was sold to Wasps on 7 October 2014 after a unanimous vote in private – less than a month after the club had returned to the Ricoh Arena.

Responding to discontent over a lack of transparency and public information about the talks prior to the sale, council leader Ann Lucas said: 'We are charged with representing you and I'm sorry that each and every decision we make can't have a referendum, but that's what democracy is about.

'You elect us and then decide whether or not we have made those decisions in your interests. We don't take our responsibilities lightly. In a decision like this, we serve the interests of the people of Coventry.'

Council officials, previously adamant that ACL's business performance had been up to scratch, admitted after the sale that the company hadn't been washing its face since the club left the stadium.

Councillor Ann Lucas told me: 'We said that ACL was profitable without the football club. The accounts show different. I fully accept that.

'The actual reality of not having the football club there for that year meant ACL couldn't wash its face.

'But we never had a problem with the company repaying its loan and they have never come to the council requesting more money.

'Would they have if we hadn't sold the company to Wasps? Who knows?'

The issue of the loan repayment was resolved shortly after the sale, with Wasps repaying the council debt in full after raising £35m through a bond scheme – a move which seriously reduced any assumed risk to the taxpayer as a result of the deal.

Wasps' acquisition of the Higgs Charity's share in ACL a few days later was slightly less straightforward. It was unclear if the football club's 'first option' to purchase the charity's share still existed following the liquidation of CCFC Ltd. To be sure, the Higgs Charity invited the club to also lodge a bid for the share – although this seemed disingenuous at best.

The club did submit a bid for the Higgs share – but the bid of almost £2.8m ultimately failed as the charity accepted a similar bid of £2.77m from Premiership rugby club Wasps, which also included a share of future ticket income.

The club had offered to invest heavily in community and educational projects as part of the deal in a vision it labelled a 'communiversity'.

A statement from the Higgs Charity explained why the organisation had turned down the club's bid.

It read: 'Notwithstanding the history of Sisu's behaviour, the Trustees considered carefully the offer to purchase made by Otium through the Joint Liquidators of CCFC Ltd.

'In addition to the financial aspects of the offers, the Trustees considered all other factors.

'Amongst other factors considered, the Wasps offer was unconditional; the Otium offer was conditional. The Wasps offer requires in effect nothing of the Trustees other than the transfer of the shares.'

Many supporters and club officials felt betrayed at the Wasps deal. There was a strong suggestion the club had been lured back to the Ricoh Arena under false pretences.

Such was the anger within Sisu that the football club's owners filed an application for a second judicial review into the Wasps deal, perhaps with a view to unravelling it at some point in the future.

Others sympathised with ACL's shareholders after the company had been heavily distressed in recent times. There had also been repeated statements from the former anchor tenant that it planned to build a new stadium and permanently leave the Ricoh Arena – something which left a huge question mark over the future of the venue and its long-term viability.

There was also an argument that the arrival of Wasps would undoubtedly benefit the local economy.

However, there is also a hugely reasonable moral argument that a council and charity which heavily criticised the owners of a football club for temporarily moving a sports team out of its home city should not have supported the owners of Wasps in its plans to permanently relocate the London rugby club.

Asked when discussions with Wasps had first started, Peter Knatchbull-Hugessen, clerk of the Higgs Charity, told me: 'During the whole of the period from before 2007, Wasps had gone through a series of different owners.

'When their brilliant plans for development in Wycombe fell away, ACL considered talking to them at that point about a ground-share, renting to a second team.

'We knew we could make it work. But nothing happened.

'Then we were trying to get the hotel sorted and dealing with Sisu. There are only so many things you can deal with at once.

'But the ground-share idea was nothing new. There had been talk of a "Sporting Club Coventry" and getting Coventry Rugby Club there too since Bryan Richardson's days.

'Those sort of ideas being kicked around are very different from serious business discussions.

'But after Sisu walked out, we started to look seriously at the sorts of things we could fill the stadium with. We even looked at monster trucks.

'From the charity's perspective, the first time we had any contact with them was around Christmas 2013 or maybe even new year 2014.

'ACL never really had any direct contact with them. It was a council and a charity matter, as shareholders in ACL.

'The deal with Wasps was agreed because the charity had a responsibility to its trustees to seriously consider offers for its shares. Sisu did put in a counter offer but it was almost designed to fail. They had no serious intention.'

Asked if the charity had any regrets about getting involved in the Ricoh Arena project, he added: 'The Ricoh Arena project is brilliant. What Wasps are doing with it is what the football club should have done.

'The rugby club now has a turnover getting on for £30m while the football club is p****** in a Johnstone's paint pot. They should be there.

'Some people have this attitude that anyone who doesn't help Sisu doesn't love the club. They can tell that to my late brother in law [Sir Derek Higgs] and my wife [Higgs Charity chairman Marilyn Knatchbull-Hugessen], who have supported the club for over 60 years, like their father before.

'That doesn't wash with me.

'I have total sadness about how it has all worked out. The football club should be there.

'With each change of leadership, since Derrick Robins, the club got further and further away from reality and further and further away from the fans.'

One conspiracy theory to emerge in the summer of 2016 was that Chris Millerchip – the former Coventry RFC player who owns the Butts Park Arena land lease (mentioned in Chapter Nine) – was in some way involved in the arrival of Wasps in Coventry and involved in a plot to force the football club out of the city.

I asked Chris Millerchip if he had been involved in attracting Wasps to Coventry, or if he had any financial interest in the Premiership rugby club. He categorically denied either, although he said he did meet Derek Richardson, the owner of Wasps, briefly on one occasion some months before the Ricoh Arena move, but was adamant that he had no influence on the decision to move to Coventry.

There has also been a suggestion that a 'City of Rugby' charity initiative being run in Coventry is also part of a move to alienate the football club. This is a scheme which aims to promote the values of rugby in schools and increase engagement in the sport.

Chris Millerchip is chairman of this project and has invested about £200,000 into it. But, looking at this objectively, it is hard to understand how this initiative could possibly be aimed at forcing the football club out of Coventry. It doesn't aim to promote rugby at the expense of football or any other sport.

Furthermore, it's a grassroots scheme that deals in things such as organising rugby tournaments for disabled schools in Coventry. It's really difficult to see how this could conceivably be part of some far-reaching evil conspiracy.

But looking for any tangible impact the arrival of Wasps had on the football team, I asked Steven Pressley about the situation in the early days – including the period when they were switched to the 'away' dressing room as Wasps took exclusive use of the 'home' dressing room.

He said: 'I don't think it had a negative effect on us. I actually preferred the dressing room we went in.

'It was smaller but the home dressing room was a dressing room we weren't able to put our own stamp on.

'When we moved into the away dressing room, its sole purpose was for the use of Coventry City.

'We were able to put our own stamp on that and I actually think that was a better situation than the cold feeling of the home dressing room.

'Although the home dressing room was used by Coventry City, it was used by other people who were utilising the stadium, so it never had that feeling of it being our own dressing room. To be fair to Wasps, they made strides to try and make things better.

'They replaced the pitch, it wasn't ideal, but it was certainly better than what we were playing on.

'They actually also put a system in place within the stadium where you could take down their branding and replace it with Coventry City branding on match day, so it would give you more of a CCFC feel.

'Although Coventry City never utilised that, Wasps did make a real effort to embrace the fact the stadium was going to be used by themselves and Coventry.'

With Wasps now in control of the stadium, I spoke to former ACL chief executive and CCFC managing director Paul Fletcher – one of the men responsible for the delivery of the project.

Asked if the club could ever be successful while Wasps owned the Ricoh Arena, he returned a damning verdict.

He told me: 'It will never work. It's a fair old middle-of-the-road. Every single penny needs to be given to the manager so he can get into this greatest league in world football.

'It's the greatest league in world football and Coventry should be there. Then the word 'Coventry' would be emblazoned all over the world and it would be great for the city, because this is a great city.

'I don't like seeing the word Coventry alongside Rochdale and Scunthorpe. I want to see Coventry alongside Manchester, Chelsea and Liverpool – that's where Coventry should be.'

Asked about his views on the current situation, which sees Wasps in control of the ground he helped build for the football club, he said: 'I have to honestly say I don't like it. When I was there, it was difficult to get the building built, but I thought if we could get the building built it had enough revenue streams to keep Coventry in the Premiership.

'That's why the Ricoh Arena was built, that's why it is there and that's why all the hotels and casinos are there; so that when Coventry got into the Premier League, all that revenue would keep them there and they wouldn't have to put the ticket prices up, as they've done at Liverpool.

'I'm sad that's not happened; it's a great building. When people talk to me about football stadiums, I think the Ricoh is as good a stadium as you can get. I'm just saddened that Coventry are not in the Premier League.'

Paul Fletcher added that finger-pointing would not help turn the club's fortunes around, and that success could only be achieved by the club owning its own ground.

Asked who was responsible for the current situation, he said: 'Have you got about 12 hours for me to give you my view on it? Probably everyone will have different views, but the thing that must happen soon is that Coventry City must own their own stadium – they just have to.

'If they don't, they will never have a chance of getting back. A message to the city – this is a fabulous city, it deserves a Premier League football club. It will only have that if Coventry City can own its own ground.'

But Mr Fletcher conceded he did not think this was a realistic aspiration.

He said: 'No, they won't build a new stadium. I don't think that would ever happen. If it did, it would be a stupid thing because I don't think the fans would follow. The fans have started to have a voice. They do have a strong voice these days.

'I loved the Coventry City fans during my time here. I thought they were fantastic and very patient. They waited until we got this great building put together.

'I think they expected better things of both their football club and their council.'

Fletcher also issued a plea to the football club's owners and the council to work together for a brighter future for the city and the football club.

He said: 'I admire Sisu for investing in the game. It's all right being critical, but they've probably lost quite a few million pounds.

'They didn't intend to do that, but sooner or later something has to happen where the football club needs to own its own stadium.

'It doesn't look good, but it has to happen if everybody in this area wants a taste of not only football matches, but football tourism.'

Another key man behind the project was then Coventry City Council development chief John McGuigan. I asked him how he felt about the way the Ricoh Arena project had turned out.

He told me: 'All the things the council said it wanted to achieve from the scheme – the regeneration, the employment opportunities, attracting businesses, changing the image of that part of the city – it did.

'The day we opened for the first football game, I overheard a woman say to her husband 'I didn't think Coventry could do anything like this.'

'The image impact was enormous. Who would have thought 15 years ago we would be seeing Take That or Bruce Springsteen playing in Coventry, or that we would be hosting Olympic football there? That is so hugely positive.

'But then, at the same time, I think what a huge opportunity lost for the football club.

'Because, certainly, they have got one of the best stadiums in the country. People come from across the world to look at it.

'The chief executive of Eden park in New Zealand came to see it two years before they hosted the Rugby World Cup to see how to generate income 365 days a year.

'The football club and successive owners have not taken the huge opportunity in front of them. From a business point of view, I just can't understand it.

'Eighty per cent of the income was not football related. I don't know why hard-nosed business people did what they did.'

The project was, of course, the vision of former club chairman Bryan Richardson. Oddly, he has never been to the arena which originally was his brainchild. Asked how he felt about the situation today, he described it as a 'tragedy'.

He told me: 'I don't know the background to everything now, but I think it's an incredible shame what has happened. Nobody has thought of the club, nobody has thought of the supporters. People have just wrecked the club. It's an absolute tragedy.'

However, he indicated his belief that the club might have a brighter future working with Ricoh Arena landlords Wasps than when Ricoh firm ACL was jointly owned by Coventry City Council and the Alan Edward Higgs Charity.

He said: 'Maybe it's better being owned by a rugby club than people who have no interest in football and no interest in Coventry City. That's the worst thing of all.

'I think it's better than having people who own that have no interest in sport – people who are only interested in it as property.

'The whole thing really was about Coventry City Football Club, then they end up going to Sixfields and you think 'what on earth has happened?'

'It's criminal really.'

Many blamed the long-serving chairman for the financial woes at the club following his departure, with reports of debts exceeding £60m widely circulated at the time.

But Mr Richardson disputes those figures to this day, and said the Ricoh Arena should have been the key to making the club self-sustainable, and blames other board members for 'destroying' the club.

He said: 'The Ricoh Arena was my brainchild. I did the deal with Tesco, we didn't use any outside agents and I did that directly with the chairman of Tesco at the time.

'I sold that 30-acre piece of land at the time for £66.5m. Well, I don't know where that money went after I'd gone. Somehow or other, the stadium was no longer ours.

'My whole idea was that the stadium would be the future of Coventry City.'

He added: 'I was demonised when I left; it's well documented. People came up with all sorts of figures that we owed. Those figures, I'm afraid, were just put out by Geoffrey Robinson [a fellow board member at the time] and his crew.

'They were so ridiculous. If he thinks anybody, any bankers are going to loan Coventry City Football Club £50m or £60m, he's mad.

'The highest-ever bank overdraft was £8m. They can verify that with the reported accounts.

'It wasn't about that; it was about people wanting to be chairman and do whatever they wanted to do. If we had held on then – we were nearly top of the Championship table at Christmas in 2001/02 – if they had held their nerve I think we would have come straight back up.'

He added: 'Would I have done anything differently? Yes, I wouldn't have had some of those people on the board. They actually destroyed Coventry City Football Club.'

Asked about what he thought the future held for the club, he said: 'I really hope Coventry City can return to the top flight. But it is damn difficult.

'It's difficult because of nothing else other than money. But you can think back and people like Southampton have done it, and done it incredibly well. Look at Bournemouth. They're the classic case of "you can do it."

'But you can't do it if you're chopping and changing every season.

'You've got to support managers. You can't just throw him out there and throw him to the wolves and say, "it's up to you, you get on with it" because that won't work,' he added.

'You can't have manager after manager and expect to do anything.

'You have to have consistency and a trust in who you have got working with you. You can't go flipping from one to another.

'I had Gordon Strachan for about six years and Ron [Atkinson] was here for two or three. Out of ten years, that's a long time.

'It's almost unheard of now. I think it's a sad reflection on the chairmen of football clubs.'

Four years ago Mr Richardson had offered his help to the existing owners – but he now says a return to the club, or football, is not something he is interested in.

He said: 'It's too late now.

'It's one of those things where while there are disparate owners, and owners who know nothing about football, you can't work that way.

'You know what should be done, but you can't do it because people won't let you get on and do the job properly.'

At the time of writing, the club's future appears to hang in the balance yet again.

The deal to return to the Ricoh Arena, signed in 2014, was a temporary arrangement, a two-year deal with an option for two more years, which was subsequently taken up.

The terms include an annual rent of £100,000 and a share of match day revenues. But club officials insist much of the income needed for the club to be viable in the long-term continue to be inaccessible.

Before this book went to print, talks over extending that deal had been frozen by Wasps, who have cited the 'background noise' of ongoing legal action by the owners of the football club as a hurdle to any long-term deal being agreed on terms more favourable to the Sky Blues.

There also seems to be little progress on any potential new stadium. This leaves Sky Blues fans facing the prospect of the club having nowhere to play by summer 2018.

David Conn, sports writer for *The Guardian*, is one of the few national journalists to have also covered the plight of the Sky Blues.

The former British Sports journalist of the year gave me his analysis of the situation.

He said: 'Football clubs are beloved institutions that people support all their lives and have a great loyalty to.

'Very often, the management and ownership of the clubs doesn't do justice to that sense of loyalty. Also, the wider governance of football – leagues and the Football Association – don't do justice to that loyalty either.

'Coventry City are a club that so many people think fondly of, probably because they were in the top flight for so long. To end up playing at Northampton Town, as a tenant, in front of 1,500 fans is arguably the worst decline of any major club that I have covered.

'It was second only to Wimbledon for the biggest boycott by supporters – an almost complete boycott. It was extremely serious. The more I looked into it, the more shocking and sad it was. The Ricoh Arena was meant to be the springboard for Coventry City into the modern era that actually solidified them as a Premier League Club.

'There were obvious financial difficulties when they moved into the Ricoh, they didn't have any money to put in and that's how the whole Higgs Charity arrangement came up.

'I would say the only other club that is comparable is Leeds – and Leeds is a catastrophic story in so many ways. But at least they are in the Championship playing at Elland Road in front of crowds in the 20,000s.

'Leeds United fans could look at Coventry City if they need to count their blessings.

'It is probably the worst in terms of calamities and the worst decline compared to a time when there has been so much money in football and local authorities have been prepared to build stadiums on really quite beneficial terms.

'It was a good vision that the arena would have all these activities in it which would self-finance things.

'The club was meant to be the owner and the long-term tenant. It was never meant to be the council and a charity having to form and operate the company. It has gone calamitously wrong, and permanently wrong with Wasps there now.

'I understand that the initial rent was a great deal of money. But at the same time, they did have a stadium built for them and in the end they hardly put in any money at all.

'Nobody was trying to screw the football club. That was the rent that they had to fix to make it stack up in the beginning.

'During all my enquiries into it, I never reached the conclusion that the council was ever trying to do anything other than regenerate an area and give its football club a massive benefit and increase its profile in an era when, if all had gone to plan, Coventry City could have gone back to the Premier League and made an absolute fortune.

'Obviously the current owners ended up in a dispute and we all know what the judges found.'

He added: 'A council in a really not well-off city, which had suffered post-industrial decline, has funded this brand spanking new stadium – and that must have been a major attraction for Sisu to buy the club in the first place.'

He added that he feared history could repeat itself if a deal with Wasps for a long-term stay at the Ricoh Arena could not be agreed.

He said: 'I think they need to stop going on about new stadiums. Play some good football and try and fill the place.

'If the owners are still not prepared to do that, then I do think there is a danger a Sixfields-type situation could happen again.

'To think that this club came to that. Tenants of North-ampton Town with the fans standing on a hill in winter to protest, or staying away completely, and to think it came about as part of a dispute. Besides everything else that was wrong about that, it was just so sad.

'This football club, with all its heritage and all the fondness people have for it, was being used as a pawn in a game that had sunk to this extent.

'Like when Wimbledon moved to Milton Keynes, it's another of those situations that the Football League has got to look at and say 'we're never going to allow that again.'

'I hope the Football League will learn lessons from it. But I think the situation at Coventry City is still very dangerous.'

I wish I could end this book on a happier note. But sadly, for now, Coventry City remains a club without a home.